Chernigov

iev

R. Dnieper

R. Don

R. Vol

R U S S I A

The Pechenegs

CRIMEA

Caucasus Mts.

lack Sea

I B E R I A

a

Caspian

Sea

Skhemaris

Valarshapat (later
Etshmiadzin)
Artishat

HYNIA

Annesi
Comana
Neocaesarea
PONTUS

Erzurum

A R M E N I A

SIA

Nyssa
CAPPADOCIA
Sebastea

Caesarea

INOR
Nazianzus
Podandos
Mts.

Taurus

Edessa

Mardin
Zafaran
Nisibis

R. Tigris

Cyprus
Salamis
Aleppo
Antioch
Homs

Mosul

Paphos

B
Lebanon
MESOPOTAMIA

Damascus

Baghdad

P E R S I A

Pelusium
Maiuma
Gaza
PALESTINE
THE
Jerusalem
HOLY LAND

iro

St. Antony's
Mountain

A R A B I A

R. Euphrates

Red Sea

R. Nile

Y P T

B Enlarged map
of the
LEBANON

Beqaa-
Kafra

Qoshayya

Batrun

Kfifan

Lebanon Mts.

Anti-Lebanon Mts.

Annaya

Bairut
Bikfaya

Damascus

Persian Gulf

CHARLES GREEN

SAINTS OF THE EAST

SAINTS
OF THE EAST

Donald Attwater

HARVILL PRESS

London

Printed in Great Britain
by Collins Clear-Type Press
London and Glasgow
for the publishers
HARVILL PRESS LIMITED
23 Lower Belgrave Street
London, S.W.1

Some of the material in this book appeared, in different form, in THE
GOLDEN BOOK OF EASTERN SAINTS published by The Bruce
Publishing Company, U.S.A., 1938

CONTENTS

ILLUSTRATIONS

Illustrations

INTRODUCTION

It is hoped that this collection of short sketches may be useful as a modest contribution to the contemporary demand amongst general readers for more information about Eastern Christianity.

The effectiveness of a people's response to Christ's call may be presented either by giving an over-all account of their general Christian life, which is a difficult thing to do, or by narrating the lives of individuals of special holiness, which is less difficult, but still not easy. One mechanical difficulty of this second method is the selection of examples that are representative—not representative of time or place (that is fairly easily ensured) but of the various avocations and states of life of men and women. It is often remarked how many known saints (note that I say *known* saints, and an exception must be made in respect of martyrs) are clergy or monks or nuns, and in the East that is perhaps even more so than in the West. I need not here examine the reasons for this; but readers may be reminded that public religious veneration, authorized by church authority (e.g., by formal canonization), is an external mark, a 'certificate', if the expression may be allowed, with which the Church honours certain individuals, a selection from among those many who contribute heroically to her holiness; and in the making of that selection some purely natural factors inevitably come into play. Furthermore, for the three centuries that the formal Roman process of

9

canonization has been in full operation, most of the East has been out of communion with the Roman see, and the very small Catholic minorities have as yet hardly come within the wider sweep of recent canonization candidates.

From early times what constitutes Christian holiness has been one of the matters wherein East and West have each applied the same principles but with differing emphases, and consequently differing results. If for a long time the categories of holiness (if holiness can have categories) were few and relatively narrow in the West, they were fewer and narrower in the East (on page 128 herein there is mention of a disagreement on this very matter between the Greeks and the early Russian Christians). All agreed on true martyrdom as a title to veneration; and after that, preference was given to bishops who were great teachers and, even more, to monks who were great ascetics. But sight was lost of the heroic virtue and faithfulness manifested by so many Christians in every walk of life, and sometimes it was even implied that the ideal of holiness which in fact the Church holds up before all men and women indiscriminately was incompatible with that secular life in which the overwhelming majority of people are, and are meant to be, engaged. So far did Easterners carry this notion, that holiness came for many of them to mean simply the life of contemplation: the complete recluse was the practical as well as the abstract ideal of a holy man. On the other hand, the saint in Russian hagiology, writes Mrs Behr-Sigel 'is a man who has the Holy Spirit and who by virtue of that gift sees—what is always there but what others do not see —the interplay between heavenly realities and earthly realities; messengers come down to him from above and he is able, sometimes, to join their supernatural insight with his own.' There is nothing narrow about that.

Actually of the twenty-four saints and other holy people written of in this book, a dozen were primarily monks, and the three lay persons were royal ('princely saints' was another Eastern category); and, since I have flicked the surface of a complex and interesting subject, I may as well give some idea of how I made my selection. *St Ignatius of Antioch* stands for all the earliest martyrs after the last of the Twelve Apostles was dead, and he is one of the few men called Apostolic Fathers. *St Basil* and *St John Chrysostom* represent the great doctors and fathers of the East, and if it be asked why them rather than Athanasius or Ephrem or John of Damascus or Gregory Nazianzen, the answer is because of the intrinsic attractiveness of their characters, because much is known about them, and because of Basil's importance in Eastern monasticism and Chrysostom as a preacher. In the same way *St Hilarion* represents the Desert Fathers, the early hermit monks of Egypt, Palestine and Syria: the choice was between him and St Antony, but St Athanasius's famous Life of Antony is available in English. *St Gregory the Enlightener* and the other early apostles of Armenia and Georgia give an opportunity of showing how early (and not so early) hagiographers made up for lack of certain knowledge by giving currency to popular exaggerations and folk tales—there has always been a tendency for some people to be more interested in miracles (and alleged miracles), a sign of holiness, than in holiness itself. *St Malchus* provides another example of the romantic tale. *St Theodore the Studite* is a most important figure in later Eastern monasticism, and *SS Athanasius the Athonite, John the Iberian* and *Euthymios the Enlightener* carried on his work and laid the foundations of the monastic republic of Mount Athos, whose religious influence has been so far-reaching and persistent. *St Pulcheria* is chosen for her intrinsic interest and also because she is characteristic as a 'royal saint', which also applies to *SS Boris* and *Gleb*. The foundations of Russian monasticism were laid by *St Theodosius Pechersky* and *St*

Sava represents the other Slav churches. *St Neilos of Rossano* is an Eastern saint in the West, *St John the Alms-giver* represents many great pastoral bishops, and *St Maximus the Confessor* is a name often met in writings about Eastern mysticism.

All these saints lived before the breach between East and West became definitive during the later Middle Ages. My last four chapters, devoted to *Mekhitar of Sivas, Bd Gabra Michael, Matthew Nakkar* and three almost contemporary Maronites, are concerned with Catholics who lived after that disastrous estrangement. The considerable number of holy men and women canonized in the Orthodox Church during the past five hundred years and more require a separate book; Mrs Nadejda Gorodetzky's *Saint Tikhon Zadonsky* (London, 1951) gives a most interesting and attractive picture of one of the more recent ones; and *Flame in the Snow* (London, 1946), by Iulia de Beausobre, is a very useful account of the characteristic Seraphim of Sarov, who died in 1833 and was canonized by the Russian synod in 1903.

I have to thank Messrs Burns & Oates Ltd. for permission to make use of some of the sketches written for the revised edition of Butler's *Lives of the Saints* (1926-38; 1956), notably Gregory the Enlightener, Hilarion and Malchus.

D.A.

ST IGNATIUS OF ANTIOCH
Martyr

'Nobis quoque peccatoribus . . .': 'We too, sinners, but your servants, put our trust in your countless mercies. Be pleased to give us a place in the fellowship of your holy apostles and martyrs, with John, Stephen, Matthias, Barnabas, *Ignatius* . . .' That prayer just before the end of the canon is familiar to everyone who has any acquaintance with the text of the Roman Mass; but there are perhaps not a few to whom this Ignatius is as much a stranger as the Alexander, Marcellinus, Peter and Anastasia among the names that follow his. Yet Ignatius of Antioch is one of the most famous of the earliest martyrs and the second of the Apostolic Fathers, so called because they lived immediately after the apostolic age.

The fame of Ignatius nowadays depends, not on what is known of his life and death (which is little), but on seven of his letters, whose text has come down to us. He was doubtless an adult convert to Christianity, and it may be that it was at baptism that he took the name Theophoros, 'God-bearer', by which he was also known. Another interpretation of this name, as 'God-borne', in time gave rise to the legend that he was the child whom Christ took in his arms, saying, 'Whoever welcomes such a child as this in my name, welcomes me . . .' Later writers say that he was a disciple of St John, but earlier ones associate him with St Peter or St Paul. He certainly became bishop of Antioch,

as the first or second successor of St Peter, who tradition-
ally was the first bishop there.

Nothing is known of Ignatius's episcopate, presumably
quite a long one, and he emerges into the light only about
the year 107 (the commonly accepted date), when he was
sentenced to death and sent to Rome for the sentence to be
carried out there: like Byron's Dacian gladiator, he was to
be 'Butcher'd to make a Roman holiday'. Even then the
light is dim: it is not known in what circumstances he was
condemned, or what exactly was the charge against him,
or by whom he was sentenced. Even in the reign of the
relatively mild Trajan the throwing of criminals to wild
beasts was so popular in Rome that provincial magistrates
had to send supplies of 'lion-fodder' to the capital. There
may have been some special reason for the singling out of
Ignatius for this treatment, but nothing is recorded about
it. Or he may have been one of a group of victims, but we
hear nothing of any such with him, at any rate before
Europe was reached.

It was a cruel journey. Ignatius wrote to the Roman
Christians: 'Just now I am in chains, learning to desire
nothing. I am fighting wild beasts all the way from Syria
to Rome, on land and sea, by day and night. I am bound
among ten leopards—I mean the squad of soldiers who
guard me: the more courteously they are treated the worse
they get.' The exact route taken, 'on land and sea', is not
certain, but Smyrna in Asia Minor was an important
stopping-place. Here he was met by the bishop, St Polycarp, and by three bishops of neighbouring cities, together
with other Christians. Among them were 'my very dear
friend Alke', a woman whose brother and nephew were to
be active in harrying Polycarp to death fifty years later.

It was from Smyrna that Ignatius wrote the first four of
his letters, three of them to the Christians of the places
whose bishops had come there to greet him, Ephesus,

Magnesia and Tralles. The fourth was to the brethren in Rome, the best-known letter of them all, and the only one that bears a date (the 9th day before the kalends of September, i.e., August 24). It had occurred to Ignatius that the more influential of them might try to get his sentence annulled, and by that 'unseasonable kindness' deprive him of the crown of martyrdom. 'I fear your love', he writes, 'lest it do me harm . . . I do not want you to seek men's favour, but to please God (as indeed you do please him); for never shall I have another such opportunity of attaining to him, and you, if you say nothing, will have the credit of a glorious achievement. . . Let my blood be poured out as an offering to him, while an altar is still ready. . . Only pray that I may have courage both in spirit and body, that I may be a resolute man and no mere talker; then I shall be a Christian in fact as well as in name. . . Let me be food for ravening animals, through which I may make my way to God.' And he uses these words that the Roman Mass has taken over for the communion chant on his feast-day: 'I am God's wheat, ground by the teeth of beasts so that I may become good bread.' (How better could he have expressed his longing to join his own self-sacrifice with that of his Master in the Eucharist?)

'It would be better', he goes on, 'to coax the animals wholly to consume me and be my tomb: then when I have fallen asleep I shall not be a burden to anybody.[1] When the world can no longer see even my body, then I shall be a true follower of Jesus Christ. Beg of the Lord that I may become a sacrifice to God through the teeth of those savage creatures. I do not give you orders, as Peter and Paul did. They were apostles; I am a convict. They were free; I am still a slave. But once I have suffered I shall be a freed man

---

[1] In later years what purported to be his mortal remains became in Rome and Antioch, not a burden, but a sacred legacy to be treasured and honoured.

of Jesus Christ, and shall rise free in him. . . Please do not interfere: I know what is good for me. I am at last beginning to be a real disciple; may nothing, seen or unseen, entice me from happily reaching Jesus Christ. Come fire or cross, struggles with fierce beasts, breaking of bones and mangling of limbs, shattering of my whole body, come all the Devil's cruellest torments on me, if only I may attain to him!'

At Troas there was a ship about to make the crossing to Macedonia, but Ignatius was able to write three more letters there. These also were to people he had met on the road, the Christians at Philadelphia and Smyrna and his friend Polycarp, bishop of the latter church. Polycarp was a young man, Ignatius a mature and experienced one, and part of the short letter consists of personal advice for the conduct of his life and office. It ends with a last request: that Polycarp will write to the chief local churches on behalf of Ignatius, who is unable to do it himself because the ship is on the point of leaving. 'Good-bye to you all, for ever in Jesus Christ our God; through him may you abide united with God and kept under his watchful eye. Farewell in the Lord!' Half a century was to pass, and then St Polycarp too was to give his life for Christ, burned at the stake in Smyrna, the first martyr (apart from St Stephen) of whose passion a full and authentic account has survived.

For it is not so in the case of St Ignatius. Like St Paul before him, he landed in Europe at Neapolis; and at the Macedonian town of Philippi he was met by the local Christians, who saw him on his way, together with others who were going to execution in chains, 'those ornaments of God's chosen ones' (who these other martyrs were and from where they came is not known; they may have been fellow prisoners with Ignatius all the time). But then darkness falls again: it can only be said that in due course Ignatius was brought to Rome and there thrown to the

16

beasts; no reliable details of his earthly end have come down to us. There is a persistent tradition that he suffered in the Flavian amphitheatre, commonly called the Colosseum, but the great hagiographical scholar Father Hippolyte Delehaye regarded even this as unproved. It is true that there are certain later accounts professing to give particulars of his sufferings and martyrdom, including a personal interview with the emperor Trajan after his arrest; but no reliance can be put on these as historical records.

The faithful who had welcomed St Ignatius at Philippi asked St Polycarp at Smyrna to send them copies of Ignatius's letters to other churches; this was done, and it may well be that we owe the preservation of the seven letters to this fact. These letters (they would take up about thirty pages of this book) are one of the most precious survivals of Christian antiquity, for what they tell us about their writer and even more for their testimony to the faith and practice, life and spirit of the Christian Church less than a century after the Lord's ascension.

A theme returned to again and again in them is the showing forth of the mystery of Christian unity by communion in faith with the bishop, obedience to his authority, and participation in the common Eucharist. To the church at Philadelphia Ignatius writes: 'All those who belong to Jesus Christ stand with their bishop. . . Make no mistake about it, brethren: anyone who follows another into schism will not inherit God's kingdom; anyone who takes up with novelties in doctrine separates himself from Christ's passion.' And again: 'Be careful to keep one Eucharist: for there is one flesh of our Lord Jesus Christ and one cup to unite us by his blood, and one altar, just as there is one bishop, together with his presbyters and deacons, my fellow servants. Thus all that you do will be done in accordance with God's will.' 'Shun divisions; from them comes evil,' he wrote to the faithful of Smyrna. 'You must all follow the bishop, as Jesus Christ followed the Father; follow the presbyters as you would the Apostles; respect the deacons as ordained by God. Let no one do anything pertaining to the church apart from the bishop. Let that be held a true Eucharist which is celebrated by the bishop, or by one whom he has appointed. Where the bishop is, there let the people be, just as where Christ Jesus is, there is the universal Church.'[1]

In the letters there are persistent warnings against the teachings of the Docetists, who at this time and place had Jewish connexions; they denied the reality of our Saviour's manhood, which they said was merely an appearance. Ignatius wrote to the brethren at Tralles: 'Refuse to listen to anyone who talks of Jesus Christ while ignoring that he was of David's line, born of Mary, really born; that he really ate and drank; that he was really persecuted under Pontius Pilate, really crucified and killed, Heaven and earth and the underworld beholding it; that he really rose from the dead, raised by his Father, and we too who believe in him the Father will raise in Christ Jesus, without whom we have no true life.' And he goes on almost in the words he uses to the Smyrneans: 'There are some unbelievers who say that he suffered only in appearance. That is not true: it is they themselves who are deluded. . . If our Lord's actions were merely make-believe, then so are my chains! Why have I given myself up to death, by fire or sword or wild beasts? Because "to be near the sword is to be near God", when the beasts are at hand, God is at hand. But it must be in the name of Jesus Christ, and thus a sharing in his passion. I endure all things because he, who became perfect man, gives me strength.' Ignatius tells the faithful

[1] *He katholike ekklesia*, the catholic church. This is the first recorded use of the expression, having here the sense of The Church at large, as a whole. St Ignatius is also the first writer to use 'Christian' as a term of honour; he was bishop of the place where it was first used at all, as a contemptuous nickname (Acts II: 26).

at Ephesus to pray without ceasing for the unconverted and to set them a good example. 'Meet their anger with gentleness, their boasting with diffidence, their abuse with prayer, their falsehoods with unshakable faith, their harshness with forbearance; and do not emulate their own example. We must show them we are their brothers by being courteous.'[1] 'Whenever Christianity is reviled by the world, what counts is not our persuasive power but its inherent greatness.'

St Ignatius's spiritual teaching revolved round the following of Christ, not stopping short of suffering and dying for him: 'Let me follow the example of the passion of my God.' Martyrdom was an ever-present reality of primitive Christian life, and what seems to us almost an obsession with it is combined in Ignatius with such joyful faith, with such passionate love for Christ, that his letters form one of the most moving documents of Christian history. He did not want torture and death: what he did want was the One whom death would give him in full. 'There is a living water gushing within me and it says "Come to the Father". I do not want perishable food or the delights of this life. I long for God's bread, which is the flesh of Jesus Christ who was of David's seed, and the drink I thirst for is his blood which is incorruptible love' (*To the Romans*).

The traditional date of the martyrdom of St Ignatius of Antioch is October 17; but in the East his feast is kept on December 20, and in the West on February 1, with a second and longer notice of him in the Roman Martyrology on December 20. This last date is perhaps that of the translation of his reputed relics from outside the walls of Antioch to the former temple of Fortune, henceforth

---

[1] But he also wrote forcefully of heretics and evil-livers. 'You must avoid them as wild beasts, they are mad dogs that bite in secret. Beware of them, their bite is hard to cure.'

known as the church of Ignatius. It is by no means sure that the martyr's relics were ever brought from Rome to Antioch (the Roman church of San Clemente claims to have them); St John Chrysostom believed that they were, but even if he were mistaken the words spoken to the Antiochenes in his homily on St Ignatius still keep their force: 'You sent him forth as a bishop, you received him back as a martyr; you sent him forth with prayers, you received him back with crowns. . . All those who come to him, this blessed Ignatius fills with blessings, with trustfulness, with a noble spirit, with sufficiency of courage, and so sends them home again.'

ST GREGORY THE ENLIGHTENER
Apostle of Armenia

The homeland of the now widely scattered Armenian people, who call themselves Hai and their country Haiastan, lies west of the Caspian Sea and south-east of the Black Sea. As well as descent from a great-great-grandson of Noah (Mount Ararat is within their borders), they claim a directly apostolic foundation for their church through the preaching of St Bartholomew and St Thaddeus, neither of which claims can be easily substantiated. Their evangelization doubtless came in fact from several directions; but they have an altogether special veneration for St Gregory (Grigor, Krikor), who began to spread the Gospel amongst them towards the end of the third century. They call him Lusavorich, which means 'the Enlightener, Light-bringer or Illuminator', or Partev, 'the Parthian'.

This Gregory was born in the middle of the third century, of uncertain origin and nationality. According to unreliable Armenian tradition he was a son of the Parthian Anak who murdered King Khosrov I of Armenia: when the dying Khosrov ordered the extermination of Anak's family, young Gregory was smuggled away by a merchant of Valarshapat to Caesarea in Cappadocia. Here he was baptized and brought up a Christian, and in due course married and had two sons, St Aristakes and St

21

Vartanes. He was eventually given a place at the court of the Armenian king Tiridates III (Tradt), which is unlikely if he were really the son of the murderer of Tiridates's father, but he soon incurred the king's displeasure by his zeal for Christianity. Active persecution began, but in the end he triumphed. Tiridates himself was converted (the Armenians venerate him as a saint, much as the Byzantines venerate Constantine) and, while Christians in the Roman empire were still suffering under the persecution of Diocletian, Christianity was proclaimed the official religion of Armenia, which thus became—superficially—the first Christian state in the world's history.

Gregory visited Caesarea and there was made bishop by the metropolitan Leontius; he established his see at Artishat on the Araxes and then set himself, with the help of Greek and Syrian missionaries, to organize his church, instruct converts and win over waverers. To recruit a clergy he took a number of youths, instructed them in the holy Scriptures, and taught them Greek and Syriac—Armenian was not yet a written language. As head of the Armenian church he sent his son Aristakes to represent him at the first general council at Nicaea in 325, and when Gregory read the proceedings of that assembly he is said to have exclaimed, 'We praise Him who was before all time, we worship the Holy Trinity and the one Godhead of the Father, the Son and the Holy Spirit, now and throughout all ages.' Whether or no St Gregory actually made use of these words they are still repeated by the celebrant in the Armenian eucharistic Liturgy after the singing of the Nicene creed.

Shortly after the council Gregory consecrated Aristakes to succeed him,[1] and retired to a hermitage on Mount Manyea in the province of Taron; in the following year,

---

[1] The chief Armenian bishop was a direct descendant of St Gregory for a century after.

about 330, he was found dead by a shepherd and was buried at Thortan, not far from Artishat.

Even these few particulars of St Gregory the Enlightener cannot be wholly relied on, but if authentic information is scarce legends are not wanting: they are set out at length in a 'history' written by one who called himself Agathangelus and averred that he was secretary to King Tiridates. Actually it was not composed earlier than the second half of the fifth century. According to this totally unreliable work, Gregory first got into trouble with Tiridates for refusing to lay a garland of flowers on the image of the goddess Anahit in her temple at Artishat. When he could not induce him to this act of idolatry, Tiridates had him tortured in twelve different ways, ways of a cruel ingenuity that differ considerably from those commonly told in legends of martyrs under the Romans. Gregory was then thrown into a noisome pit, stinking with corpses, filth and vermin, where he was left and forgotten for fifteen years. He was kept alive by the ministrations of a kindly widow.

Meanwhile Tiridates went on persecuting, and among his victims were St Rhipsime, St Gaiana, and their companions. Although these maidens, apparently the protomartyrs of the Armenian church, are known to have been venerated from early times (they are mentioned in the Roman Martyrology on September 29 as having suffered under King Tiridates), there is no reliable information about their history or the circumstances of their passion. The legends related by Agathangelus and others are romance of the most barefaced kind. They narrate that Rhipsime was a girl of noble birth, one of a community of consecrated virgins at Rome presided over by Gaiana. The emperor, Diocletian, having made up his mind to marry, sent a painter round the city to paint the portraits of all those ladies who seemed to him eligible, and he did his work with such conscientious thoroughness that he penetrated into the house of Gaiana and made likenesses of some of her maidens.

When Diocletian examined the portraits his choice fell on Rhipsime, and she was duly informed of the honour that had befallen her. It was not at all to her liking, and Gaiana was so afraid of what the emperor might do at this refusal that she gathered her flock together, went aboard ship, and sailed to Alexandria. From there they made their way through the Holy Land to Armenia, where they settled down in the royal city of Valarshapat and earned their living by weaving. The beauty of Rhipsime soon attracted attention, but the noise of their arrival apparently reached Rome before it came to the ears of King Tiridates, for Diocletian wrote asking him to kill Gaiana and send Rhipsime back—unless he would like to keep her for himself. Thereupon Tiridates sent a deputation to fetch her to his palace, but when it arrived at her house, and Rhipsime appealed to Heaven for help, so fierce a thunderstorm at once broke out that the horses of the courtiers became unmanageable and they were all thrown into hopeless confusion. When Tiridates heard this and that the girl refused to come, he ordered her to be brought by force, and when she was led into his presence he was so attracted that he tried to embrace her on the spot. Rhipsime not only resisted but threw the king ignominiously to the floor, and in a rage he ordered her to prison. But she escaped and returned to her companions during the night.

At morning when they found her gone the king sent soldiers after her with orders that she was to be put to death, and all the other maidens with her. St Rhipsime was roasted alive and torn limb from limb, and St Gaiana and

St Ignatius
of Antioch

*Monastery of
Chevetogne*

St Gregory, St Basil and St John Chrysostom, the Three Holy Hierarchs of the Greek Church, from the twelfth-century mosaic in the Capella Palatina, Palermo

St Theodore
the Studite

*Monastery of
Chevetogne*

the rest to the number of thirty-five were likewise brutally slain; only one, St Nino, escaped.[1]

Retribution was lying in wait for Tiridates. A week later, while out hunting, he was turned into the likeness of a wild boar and went roaming about the woods with others of his kind. Then it was that his sister had a vision: she was told that fifteen years before a holy man named Gregory had been thrown down a pit, that he was still alive, and that through him alone could her royal brother be restored to his natural shape. Accordingly the pit was searched, St Gregory was found and brought out, and at his prayer Tiridates recovered his right mind and body; in repentance the king, his wife and his sister were all baptized.

After this, we are told, St Gregory fasted, prayed and preached with great vigour (with such vigour that, though the false gods had to be opposed by force of arms, he baptized four million people in seven days), and at the end of seventy days he, too, had a vision. He seemed to see the skies open and our Lord come down to earth in glory, carrying a hammer of gold with which he struck the ground; thereupon arose from the place a high shining pillar, with a cross at the top, and around were three smaller pillars, the colour of blood; covering them there appeared a great church from which flowed a stream which formed a lake, and into this lake there passed numbers of black goats which came out the other side as white sheep. And Gregory knew that this represented the chief church of Armenia which God wanted built there, and that its fame should overtop even that of St Rhipsime and St Gaiana and their fellows, represented by the red pillars. So he built the church and the place was called Etshmiadzin,

[1] Father Paul Peeters, who studied the legend closely, declared that 'It would perhaps be going too far to deny the existence of these martyrs . . .'

which means 'the Only-begotten has come down', and to this day it is the chief episcopal see of the Armenian Church. But it became so only after the days of St Gregory, and his vision is probably a story invented to bolster up the claim of the Armenian Church to be independent of the metropolitan of Caesarea. One cannot but regret that some of these extravagant tales should still receive recognition in the Armenian calendar.

The Roman Martyrology names St Gregory on his traditional day, September 30, and, curiously enough, devotion to him is found in southern Italy, introduced there by Armenian immigrants. A church in Naples actually claims to have relics of him; but, though the Greeks say his remains were translated to Constantinople (where he was venerated as a martyr), it is unlikely that they ever left Armenia.

It is mentioned above that one of St Gaiana's maidens, Nino, was said to have escaped with her life, and she is identified by the Iberians with the heroine of a story told by Rufinus in his version of the *Ecclesiastical History* of Eusebius. He says that early in the fourth century a maiden was carried off captive into Iberia (Georgia, north of Armenia; now in the U.S.S.R.) who made a great impression on the people there by the sobriety and purity of her life and the long hours she gave to prayer. When questioned, she simply told them that she worshipped one Jesus Christ as God.

One day a mother brought her sick child to Nino, asking how it ought to be treated. Nino told her that Christ was able to heal the most desperate cases, and, wrapping the child in her mantle, she called on the name of the Lord and gave the baby back in perfect health. Rumours of this came to the queen of Iberia, who was herself ill, and she sent for Nino; when Nino declined to come (the early Christians were shy of royal courts), the queen had herself carried to her, and she also was cured. When she would have thanked and rewarded her benefactress she was told that, 'It is not my doing but Christ's; he is the Son of God and you ought to pray to him, for it is to him that you owe your life and health.' The queen reported these words to her husband who, when he soon after got lost in a heavy fog while hunting, swore that if this Christ were God and would show him his way home he would believe in him. Instantly the fog cleared; and the king kept his word. He and his wife were taught by St Nino, he announced his change of religion to the people, and began to build a church. In the course of its building God wrought another miracle at the word of St Nino, for a pillar, which neither men nor oxen had been able to raise, reared itself upright and, after remaining suspended in the air, settled itself in its right place, all before the eyes of a large crowd. The king sent an embassy to the emperor Constantine, telling him what had happened and asking that priests might be sent to Iberia, which was duly done: 'The emperor was more gladdened by this news than if he had annexed unknown peoples and kingdoms to the Roman empire.'

Rufinus learned this story from an Iberian prince whom he met in Palestine before the beginning of the fifth century, and in Georgian literature there is a whole cycle of Nino legends, which are worthless as history. Rufinus gives no localities for his events or the name of the king and queen concerned or even the name of the Christian girl—much less her nationality or place of origin. Later versions supply these omissions several times over. Nino (sometimes said to have been not a captive slave but a voluntary fugitive from the persecution of Diocletian) came from Cappadocia—and also from Rome, Jerusalem and the Franks: the Armenians, as we have seen, make her an Armenian and associate her with St Rhipsime.

After seeing Christianity firmly established in the land,

Nino is said to have retired to a hermitage on a mountain at Bodbe in Kakheti. Here, ministered to by a Bishop John, she died and was buried; later the place was made an episcopal see and her tomb is still shown. It is interesting to note that from time immemorial the cathedral of Metzkheta has been known as the church of the Living Pillar. Iberia had many Christians at the time Rufinus wrote, but what was the truth behind the story he heard from the Iberian prince (and even what exactly that story itself was) it is now impossible to say. The evangelization of Iberia must have come from more than one direction. About the middle of the sixth century, for example, a band of thirteen Syrian monks came into the Caucasus country, led by St John Zedazneli, and made the beginning of that intense monastic life for which the early Christian centuries in Iberia were notable.

St Nino is mentioned in the Roman Martyrology on December 15; but as Rufinus does not give her name she is referred to simply as *sancta Christiana ancilla*, 'St Christiana, a maidservant'.

ST BASIL THE GREAT
*Doctor of the Church and Father
of Eastern Monks*

Basil the Great was born at Caesarea in Cappadocia
(eastern Asia Minor) towards the end of the year 329,
into a family that was distinguished and wealthy and
Christian, whose distinction was religious as well as
secular. His grandfather and grandmother, the latter
known as St Macrina the Elder, had suffered considerably
during the persecutions; his father, also called Basil and
venerated as a saint, was a professor of oratory at Caesarea
and one who did not disdain the classics of pagan Greece;
his mother, St Emmelia, daughter of a martyr, was gracious
in mind and body. Basil the Elder and Emmelia had ten
children, five boys and five girls, the eldest of all being
known in history as St Macrina the Younger; the third
boy was St Gregory, afterwards bishop of Nyssa and a
father of the Church, and another younger son, St Peter,
became bishop of Sebastea.

In this remarkable family Basil junior was the eldest son,
born a year after Macrina. From the beginning he was
delicate and suffered from ill-health all his life; most of his
earliest years seem to have been spent at his family's
country house near Neocaesarea (now called Niksar) in
Pontus, which was the district stretching along the south-
east coast of the Black Sea. Here he was brought up by his
grandmother and his mother, and 'I shall never forget', he

says, 'the deep impression that the words and example of
these venerable women made on me when I was a boy.'
The rudiments of secular education, reading, writing,
logic (what is the good of learning to read and write without learning how to reason?), were given him by his father,
for recreation there were riding and hunting and fishing
in the mountains, and then when he was about sixteen he
was sent to study at the public schools—which were more
like universities: first at Caesarea (now Kayseri), which
was the metropolis of Cappadocia, then at the new imperial city of Constantinople, and finally at Athens, where
he met one Gregory, a young man a few years older than
himself from Nazianzus.[1]

The ancient paganism of Hellas was not yet dead and
Athens was its heart, so that the city was dangerous enough
religiously and morally for young Christians, especially
such as were too intelligent to be 'superior' and ob-
scurantist towards its classical learning. Among his fellow
students Basil in fact met that young prince who was to
become emperor and go down to posterity as Julian the
Apostate. Watching and listening to him in those early
days Basil said, 'See what a scourge the empire is preparing
for itself.' But Basil and Gregory of Nazianzus had struck
up a firm friendship, and together they armed themselves
against the surrounding dangers by spending in church
most of the time that they were not working.[2] Their studies
included logic, philosophy, poetry, history, geometry and

---

[1] St Basil, St Gregory of Nyssa, St Gregory Nazianzen—the three
Cappadocian Fathers.

[2] In his panegyric of Basil, Gregory Nazianzen recalls these days, and
in speaking of an amusing quarrel between Armenian and Cappadocian students makes that remark about the Armenians that has
haunted them ever since: 'I do not find the Armenians a noble race;
they are very sly and vicious.' Schoolboy intolerance of near
neighbours.

mathematics, astronomy, medicine, and when at the age of twenty-five Basil left Athens to become a teacher of rhetoric at Caesarea he was, testifies Gregory, already well known for the steadiness of his character and the brilliance of his mind, equipped 'with all the learning attainable by the nature of man'.

It may surprise us to learn that all this time Basil was not yet baptized, according to the custom common in those days which put off baptism till mature years, or even till the hour of death.[1] But his sister Macrina (who since the untimely death of the man whom she was to have married had made up her mind to dedicate herself in maidenhood) had been watching him, and she was rather disturbed: there were signs that Basil's success and popularity were going to his head, he was 'puffed up beyond measure by his oratorical powers; he looked down on the most learned and distinguished of his neighbours'. She prayed, and she talked to him—and in 357 he resolved to become a monk, having been baptized by his old friend Dianeios, bishop of Caesarea. 'I was like one awakened from a deep sleep,' he wrote. 'I saw the wondrous light of Christian virtue; I realized the futility and emptiness of the wisdom of the great ones of this world, which passes and perishes. . . I read the gospel and learned there that the high road to perfection is to sell all that one has and share with the poor, to give up worrying about earthly things, to refuse to allow the soul to be distracted by love of them.'

When it is said that Basil resolved 'to become a monk' it does not at all mean what those words mean today, that is, membership in a community, living a highly organized life together under one roof and subject to the same rule. In 357 there were many Christian monks, but no

---

[1] For example, Constantine the Great, the first Christian emperor, received baptism only on his deathbed. Both Basil and Gregory Nazianzen afterwards wrote strongly against this custom.

monasteries as we understand the term, or any fixed monastic rule either. A monk[1] was a solitary, living generally in a remote place and spending his time in religious contemplation and providing for his small material wants by growing his food, and so forth; at the most he was a member of a colony of hermits, living in separate cells, and owing a loose allegiance to a senior of recognized experience and holiness; they were not priests, they had no vows. St Basil spent some time after his baptism travelling from one centre to another of these solitaries and hermits, visiting Egypt (where St Pachomius had died ten years earlier after making the first successful experiments in organized monasticism), Palestine, Syria and Mesopotamia. He admired the monks' austerity, their watchings in prayer at night, their perseverance, 'the high and noble spirit that made them disregard hunger and thirst and cold, as if they were free from the body and already citizens of Heaven', but he did not settle down with any of them: he had his own ideas about monastic life, and he returned to Pontus to see if he could carry them out.

His widowed mother Emmelia and his sister Macrina with some friends had already retired to live a communal life at a beautiful place called Annesi on the river Iris (Yesil Irmak), and he took up his abode on the opposite bank; he invited Gregory of Nazianzus to join him there. Gregory was wanted at home and suggested instead that the other should come to Nazianzus, but Basil would not leave the beauty and quietness of Annesi for a place which, he said, was full of bears and wolves and mud, and repulsive to look at. Gregory did come later on for a time, but Basil's first disciple was his brother Peter, and soon his followers had grown into a large community

---

[1] The word *monk* is from Greek *monakhos*, from *monos*, alone, single.

which Basil organized as the first monastery in Asia Minor.

St Basil lived the life of a monk in the strict sense for only five years, but in the history of Christian monachism he ranks in importance with St Benedict himself, and his 'new range of ideas' cannot be better summarized than in the words of that great Benedictine, Abbot Cuthbert Butler:

'St Basil established a common roof, a common table and common prayer always: so that we meet here for the first time in Christian monastic legislation the idea of the *cenobium*, and common life properly so called. Again, St Basil declared against even the theoretical superiority of the eremitical life over the cenobitical. He asserted the principle that monks should endeavour to do good to their fellow men; and in order to bring works of charity within reach of his monks, orphanages were established, separate from the monasteries but close at hand and under the care of the monks, in which apparently children of both sexes were received. Boys also were taken into the monasteries to be educated, and not with the view of their becoming monks. Another new feature in St Basil's conception of the monastic life was his discouragement of excessive asceticism; he enunciated the principle that work is of greater value than austerities, and drew the conclusion that fasting should not be practised to such an extent as to be detrimental to work.' The monks were still not priests (nor are they usually now in the East, and not till long after St Basil's time in the West), and there were still no vows, but he established a period of probation and there was a strict obligation of perseverance. 'Their time was divided between prayer, work and the reading of Holy Scripture. They rose for the common psalmody while it was still night and chanted the divine praises till the dawn; six times each day did they assemble in the church of prayer.

Their work was field labour and farming—St Gregory Nazianzen speaks of the plowing and vine-dressing, the wood-drawing and stone-hewing, the planting and draining. The food and clothing, too, the housing and all the conditions of life, he describes as being coarse and rough and austere. The monastic virtues of obedience to the superior, of personal poverty, of self-denial, and the cultivation of the spiritual life and of personal religion are insisted on.'[1]

The likeness of the above to the spirit and practice of the Rule of St Benedict is at once apparent, and Abbot Butler declares that 'St Benedict, though he borrowed more in matter of detail from Cassian, in matter of principles and ideas owed more to St Basil than to any other monastic legislator'. As for the monks of the East, they all, with small exceptions, look on Basil as their patriarch and father among the saints, though they have departed from his practice in the matter of orphanages and schools and similar works. The reading and study that he imposed were for spiritual rather than theological ends, and there have been times and places when his followers, unlike, for example, St Theodore the Studite, have looked on intellectual pursuits as unworthy of their calling, indeed as a worldly snare. St Basil's views on the bringing up of boys are of interest: 'Education,' he says, 'should be pleasant, attractive and tranquillizing to the mind, leading the pupil on without constraint and without tiring him'; punishment should be specially moderate when it is in respect of faults in lessons, but vicious habits must be severely dealt with; no part of the monastic rule was to be applied to the boys' lives, and any who showed special aptitude were allowed to attend the classes of expert masters outside the house. But it must be understood that

[1] *The Cambridge Medieval History*, ed. Gwatkin and Witney, Vol. 1, pp. 528, 529.

the so-called Rule of St Basil was not so much legislative as supplementary to the way of life which was being actually led in his monastery: the two parts were drawn up in the form of questions and answers, which deal in the main with the virtues and vices and aim at the inculcation of the religious spirit; practical details of life and administration were left to the local superiors.

During these years the Church was going through a very critical period. The Arian heresy[1] was at its height, the emperor Constantius trying to impose it and persecuting the orthodox. After his death came the episode of Julian's attempt to revive paganism, in the course of which Caesarea was one of the Christian cities that specially incurred his wrath. Its bishop, Eusebius, was not capable of dealing with the general situation, and to help him Basil was in 363 persuaded to go to Caesarea and be ordained deacon and priest; soon afterwards, finding that the bishop was jealous of his influence, he returned to Annesi. But when the Arian Valens became co-emperor and things were looking black, Basil went back to Caesarea and was accepted by Bishop Eusebius as a sort of vicar general, and for the next five years he was the great power in the diocese: 'The one,' says St Gregory, 'led the people, the other led their leader.' It was perhaps at this time that he did work on the services of the church of Caesarea, giving rise to that Liturgy of St Basil which is still used on certain days of the year in churches of Byzantine rite.

But what drew the hearts of the people to him more than anything else was his activity during the famine of 367-68. The magistrates lost their heads and did nothing, and those that were able hoarded and profiteered; Basil sold

---

[1] The belief that the Son is inferior to the Father and of a different substance, i.e., not true God at all. One of the most widespread and devastating heresies that ever afflicted the Church.

what was left of his own extensive property for the benefit of the starving and sick, he raised subscriptions and organized the work of relief (forbidding any distinction to be made between Christians and Jews), he cajoled and threatened the profiteers till they disgorged, and then he rounded on the rich who would not help: without any circumlocution or legalistic finesse he told them that all the goods that are superfluous to a Christian's own reasonable needs belong to his hungry and naked neighbours. Then the bishop, Eusebius, died and Basil was put forward as his successor; there was opposition and Gregory the Elder, bishop of Nazianzus, a very old man, came to his support; to those who pointed out that Basil's health was weak he retorted 'So it is. But we want a religious teacher and leader, not an athlete.'[1] So St Basil was elected, and was consecrated on 14 June 370; he was only about forty years old.

Caesarea was much more than a simple bishopric or metropolitan see; it was more like what later was called in the West a primatial see, its bishop having higher jurisdiction over the dioceses of nearly all eastern Asia Minor, and over the church of Armenia: it was one of the half dozen greater sees in the Eastern church at that time, and was rendered even more powerful and respected by the genius of St Basil. Almost at once after his election he had to cope with violent persecution against orthodox Christians from the Arian emperor Valens, and he was summoned before the representative of the civil power, the praetorian prefect Domitius Modestus, who asked him how he had the audacity to disobey the emperor and preach against Arian doctrine.

'I don't understand you,' replied Basil. 'What audacity and disobedience are you talking about?'

---

[1] Gregory the Elder was the father of Basil's friend, the other Gregory of Nazianzus.

'You do not accept the emperor's religion; yet every-body else does.'

'My Emperor forbids me to. I cannot give divine wor-ship to any creature of God.'

'What about us then?' retorted the prefect. 'Aren't we good enough for you?'

'I do not deny that you are magistrates and important people,' Basil replied. 'And I should be honoured by your friendship. But the test of Christianity is faith, not worldly position.'

Then Modestus began to threaten, and asked Basil if he wasn't afraid.

'Why should I be afraid? What can happen to me?'

'What can happen to you? You can lose your property and be banished. Torture. Death.'

'Try something else,' said Basil imperturbably. 'These things don't worry me.'

'Nobody has ever dared talk to me like this before,' fumed the outraged prefect, to which Basil suggested that perhaps he had not had much to do with true bishops.[1]

The upshot was that the emperor himself came to Caesarea to interview this recalcitrant prelate, and there are stories told of signs from Heaven on the bishop's behalf. What is certain is that Basil treated him firmly but with proper respect. When at Epiphany in 372 the emperor presented himself at the Holy Mysteries to make his offering it was not refused. Basil received it with his own hands. Henceforward Valens was in two minds about this bishop, and made only half-hearted attempts to inter-fere with his campaign against Arianism, a campaign carried on by sermons and writings that were one of the

---

[1] This from a man who, as St Gregory Nazianzen tells us, was habitually shy and absorbed in his own thoughts.

most powerful agents in completing the work of St Athanasius.

The care for the poor which he had shown during the great famine was continued by Basil when he himself was bishop. He established a large institution where strangers could find a welcome, the needy sick be treated, and training in tradesmanship be given to the unskilled; nor was he silent when the well-to-do failed in their duty. 'You refuse to give under the pretext that you haven't got enough for your own requirements,' he exclaimed in one of his sermons. 'But while your tongue excuses, your hand condemns—that ring shining on your finger silently declares you to be a liar! How many debtors could be released from prison with one of those rings? How many ill-clad people could be clothed from one only of your wardrobes? And yet you turn the poor away empty-handed.' But he did not confine the obligation of giving to the rich alone. 'You are poor? But there are others poorer than you. You have enough to keep you alive for ten days —but this man has enough for only one. . . . Don't be afraid to give away the little that you have. Don't put your own interests before the common need. Give your last loaf to the beggar at your door, and trust in the goodness of God.' And he required that common sense should be used in almsgiving: 'It is useless to give a lot to those people who make up pitiful tales to appeal to women, or make a show of their deformities and diseases—undue generosity may even be an occasion of sin to them. Meet their importunities with a small alms, and keep your sympathy for those who carry their misfortunes more modestly.' St Basil had to be particularly severe about usurers, 'who speculate in public want, who sow where they have no land and reap where they have not sown'—'I have seen free men put up their children for sale in the market place in order to repay money-lenders; it is a ghastly sight.'

Much of the extent and variety of Basil's activity can be seen in his letters, of which a fascinating collection of 365 has survived. From clergy and laity alike he required exact discipline, and he tells of his difficulties with a foolish young deacon (Basil alludes to him ironically as 'grave and reverend') who went about with a troop of girls and was the cause of much disorder; he had to deal with simony in ecclesiastical offices and the reception of unfit persons among the clergy; he stood up against the rapacity and oppression of officials, and excommunicated all those concerned in the 'white-slave traffic' which was widespread in Cappadocia; he could rebuke with dreadful severity, but he preferred the way of gentleness: there is the letter to the dedicated maiden who had strayed, and the one to an ecclesiastic in a responsible position who was mixing himself up in politics; and thieves, expecting to be handed over to the magistrates and a stiff sentence, were often sent away free—but with a lively admonishment ringing in their ears. 'The physical punishments of the courts will never cure these fellows,' said the bishop, 'but perhaps the fear of God will.' A letter to a bishop who had slandered him is a model of dignified protest. 'Many visitors here from Ancyra,' he begins, 'tell me that you, a man dear to me—how can I put it without giving offence?—that you do not speak of me in a very pleasant way nor in the terms that I should expect from such a man as yourself. . . Would it have been asking too much of you, dear sir, to write me a short letter as between friends, setting out the matters that trouble you? Or alternatively to get me to come and see you? . . . It would be a help to me if you would tell me frankly why you are offended with me.' Most of the longer letters deal with weighty matters of doctrine and discipline, and it is noticeable how few references there are to current 'world-events' and imperial affairs.

On one occasion Basil gave shelter in his house to a

young widow who was threatened with kidnapping by a
prefectorial official. The prefect was furious, not with his
subordinate but with Basil, who was summoned to his
court to give an account of his action. The news ran round
the city and, says St Gregory Nazianzen, the people
streamed out of their houses 'like a swarm of bees smoked
out of their hive', and demonstrated angrily outside the
court-house. The prefect was thoroughly frightened and
appealed to the bishop to calm the mob. Without a word,
he signalled for a gangway to be made and the prefect
passed through the people untouched and in silence, Basil
following, not, probably, without a slightly ironical smile
on his face.

St Basil was a man of many friends: 'From youth to old
age,'[1] he himself wrote, 'I have had many friends... I have
never sinned against friendship.' We have already seen his
close association with Gregory of Nazianzus, and that was
beyond question the great friendship of his life. But for
a period towards the end there was an unhappy coolness, at
any rate on Gregory's side, that arose in this way. A great
deal of trouble was caused to Basil by an ambitious bishop
in his province, Anthimos of Tyana, and Basil planned to
neutralize the effect of his insubordination by putting
specially reliable bishops in charge of the dioceses neighbouring Tyana. So in 371 he ordained his brother Gregory
for the see of Nyssa (he proved to be not at all an effective
bishop), and invited Gregory of Nazianzus to be bishop of
Sasima. Now this Gregory had only with great unwilling-
ness become a priest, and he flatly refused to be a bishop.
Whereupon Basil did what would seem to be a wholly un-
justifiable thing: he insisted on his friend's consecration
against his will. St Gregory's indignation is understandable: he swore he would not go near Sasima, nor did he;
first he fled to the mountains, then he came back to

[1] This is a manner of speech: he was barely fifty when he died.

Nazianzus to help his dying father, then he became a hermit at Seleucia in Isauria, outside Basil's province, and in all these seven years the disagreement was not mended. This is the outstanding, though not the only, example in Basil's life of a certain headstrongness, and its results were deplorable; after his death, however, St Gregory repented of his own conduct: he preached a great panegyric of his old friend in 381, and began the collection of his letters for which we are so indebted to him.

The trouble with Bishop Anthimos of Tyana that led to these events had its origin in the making of Tyana the capital of a new civil province, the choice of that city being due to an action of St Basil which shows his concern for the temporal prosperity of the people. Valens had decided to carve a new province out of Cappadocia: this was a common dodge to increase taxability, and in this case (as in others) involved the compulsory transfer of a number of citizens of standing to the capital of the new province. This was a nasty little town, at the foot of the Taurus mountains, called Podandos, and the citizens threatened with exile to this place came to beseech the help of their bishop. Would he go to Constantinople and try to dissuade the emperor? For more than one reason Basil did not judge it expedient to do this, but he promised to write to influential friends at the capital and see what could be done. He did so, and a pleasantly rhetorical letter it is: 'The meetings and discussions of intellectual people for which this city [Caesarea] was formerly famous are now a thing of the past. . . Nothing is heard but yells of inspectors of taxes and the groans of their tortured victims: these sounds alone echo along the deserted colonnades. The baths and gymnasia are shut, and the streets are not lit at night. . . Some of the wealthy folk have fled, they prefer exile to Podandos; others, including most of the officials, have already been taken there, with their wives and families—

41

a distressing sight for their friends. Those that are left
behind, bewailing the fate of their relatives and friends and
unable to meet the demands of the tax people, find their
life not worth living. It is as if there had been an earthquake or flood—the city has so changed that you would
not recognize it.'

No doubt after receiving such an appeal Basil's agents
in Constantinople did their best, but they did not have
much success; the emperor was unmoved by Basil's just
observation that 'the government cannot make two horses
by cutting one horse into two'. The only concession he
would make was that the capital of the new province
should be at Tyana instead of the hated Podandos. And
accordingly Bishop Anthimos thought his see should now
be the equal of Caesarea, which led to a great deal of un-
pleasantness all round, and indirectly to the breach between
Basil and Gregory of Nazianzus.

Outstanding among St Basil's other friends was St
Eusebius, bishop of Samosata, another vigorous opponent
of Arianism, who for this cause was turned out of his see
by Valens. At the time of Basil's death he was hoping to be
restored to it, and the letter Basil sent referring to this may
have been the last he ever wrote. 'If I live,' he said, 'may
it please Almighty God to let me see so happy an event,
or if I cannot, then may those many people who look on
your return as their hope of salvation. I feel sure that the
time will come when the God of mercy, moved by the tears
which are shed for you in all the churches, will send you
back safe and sound to those who are ceaselessly praying
for you.'[1] Another friend was St Amphilochius, a cousin of
Gregory of Nazianzus, who as a younger man had been a
lawyer at Constantinople and got into trouble about money.

[1] A few months after Basil's death Eusebius was killed by an Arian
woman who threw a tile at his head from a housetop; the Roman
Martyrology calls him a martyr (June 21).

In 375 St Basil nominated him bishop of Iconium (now Konia), and Amphilochius consulted him on cases of conscience, to which we have the replies, which form almost a treatise on canon law. A charming story is told of how St Ephrem came all the way from Mesopotamia to see the great bishop of Caesarea. According to a writing attributed to Ephrem himself, St Basil was presiding at a service in church when he arrived, and 'I heard the teaching of St Paul, the law of the gospel, the religious awe of our mysteries pouring from his mouth: I saw that holy assembly all shining with divine grace'. After the office Basil came to greet Ephrem and said to him (by an interpreter, for neither could speak the other's language), 'Are you Ephrem, who has taken the yoke of salvation upon himself so excellently?'

And St Ephrem replied: 'I am Ephrem who walks unworthily in the way of salvation.' And they kissed one another.

But not all St Basil's friends were worthy of his love and affection, or could say with him, 'I have never sinned against friendship'. The saddest example was that of Eustathius of Sebastea who had been intimate with Basil for years. He not only turned Arian, but spread shameful slanders against his old associate, in spite of all Basil's characteristically gentle efforts to reclaim him. 'I am tempted to despair of human nature,' he wrote, 'to believe it incapable of affection, when I think that this man, virtuous throughout his life, should be so carried away as to forget what he knows of me and to believe such tales.'

St Basil wrote to St Athanasius that 'the only safe way for the churches of the East is to have the sympathy of the churches of the West,' but Basil himself failed in his appeals to Pope St Damasus and other Western bishops to help straighten out difficulties in the East arising from the

Arian struggle. He was apparently misunderstood and misrepresented in Rome; on the other hand, he did not always express himself tactfully. 'For my sins, I seem to fail in everything,' he groaned. But a letter to St Ambrose (the two considerably resembled one another) when he was made bishop of Milan in 374 is one more example of Basil's friendly and affectionate nature. 'God chooses those who are pleasing to him. He put a shepherd at the head of his people, and of the goat-herd Amos he made a prophet. . . It is not from men, O man of God, that you have learned the good news of Christ; it is the Lord himself who took you from among the Roman magistrates to put you in the chair of the apostles. Fight the good fight. . . Do not forget often to write to me, so that our friendship may remain strong and we may be always neighbours in spirit although a great distance divides us on earth.'

It is astonishing that all the work of St Basil's episcopate was done within a period of nine years and under the handicap of persistent ill-health; he was so pale and thin that Gregory of Nazianzus said he seemed to have scarcely any flesh or blood left. Yet he did not relax those habits of austerity he had learned as a monk, nor did he allow the cares of a large province to distract him from 'the one thing necessary'. The impression he made on St Ephrem when conducting a service in church has been mentioned, and a passage in a letter to a patrician lady named Caesaria throws interesting light on the practice of Basil's own household in the matter of the Lord's Supper: 'To receive Christ's holy body and blood every day is good and healthful, for he himself said that those who eat his flesh and drink his blood shall have eternal life. . . I communicate four times a week, on Sunday, Wednesday, Friday and Saturday, and on other days if the feast of a saint is celebrated.' From the bishop's house at Caesarea there went forth an influence that did not stop short at the borders of his diocese or with the earthly end of its source; by common consent St Basil is recognized as one of the greatest figures in Christian history, meet, indeed, to be called 'the Great', one who, being dead, yet speaketh. And it is difficult to know in which aspect to admire him most, as the perfect model of a bishop, as a doctor of the Church, as a monk and the father of countless monks—but there is no need so to divide him: he was one man, the man who wrote the letters.

In the year 373 St Basil was at death's door, and he seems never really to have recovered; he refers to the ineffectual hot baths at medicinal springs that had been prescribed ('warmth is no good to the dead'), and a year or two later to the uselessness of his teeth. He died on 1 January 379, whilst crowds were praying for him in the street outside. All Caesarea was present at his burying in 'the tomb of his fathers', Jews and heathen as well as Christians, and strangers from outlying parts. Shortly after presiding at the funeral, St Gregory of Nyssa went to Annesi to comfort their sister St Macrina, who was ill—but she would not mourn for Basil: was he not with God?

Gregory had been a sharp critic of his brother in his earlier days, but now he said of him, 'Paul came before him in time, Basil followed generations later, but this is God's dispensation for men and not a proof of lesser excellence. Moses was born long after Abraham, Samuel after Moses, and then Elias; later still came the great John, after him Paul, and after Paul Basil.' Seventy-two years later the Council of Chalcedon referred to him as, 'the great Basil, a minister of grace who expounded truth to the whole world'.

In the East St Basil the Great is one of the Three Holy Hierarchs, the others being St John Chrysostom

and St Gregory Nazianzen, to whom the West adds St
Athanasius to make up the four great Greek doctors. The
Byzantines keep his feast on the day of his death and
the Latins on June 14, the anniversary of his episcopal
ordination.

ST HILARION
A Father of the Desert

During the second half of the fifth century the centre
of Christian monasticism had shifted from Egypt to
Palestine, where St Theodosius the Cenobiarch exercised
a general supervision over all monasteries of communal
life and St Sabas over the semi-eremitical ones (*lauras*): the
seed of this flowering, the first known hermit in Palestine,
was St Hilarion, whose feast is kept on October 21.

He was born at a village called Tabatha, five miles to
the south of Gaza, about the year 291; his parents were
pagans and they sent the boy to Alexandria to be educated.
Here he became a Christian, being baptized when he was
about fifteen; and having heard of St Antony, who was
famous throughout Egypt, he went into the desert to see
him. Hilarion stayed with him two months, studying his
manner of life, but he found the desert only less distracting
than the town, for crowds flocked to Antony's cell; so,
wanting to serve God in perfect solitude, he returned to his
own country. Finding his father and mother both dead, he
gave away his goods to the poor, keeping nothing for himself (for he was mindful of Ananias and Sapphira, says St
Jerome), and about the year 307 retired into the desert
seven miles from Maiuma, near Gaza, between the sea-
shore on one side and a swamp on the other, a place
notorious for murders and robberies.

Hilarion was a good-looking, delicate youth, easily

47

affected by the least excess of heat or cold, yet for clothing he wore a shirt of sackcloth, a leather tunic which St Antony had given him, and an ordinary short cloak. He cut his hair only once a year, did not change a tunic till it was worn out, and never washed the sackcloth which he had once put on, thinking it 'idle to look for cleanliness in a hair shirt'; which mortifications, Alban Butler remarks with his usual pertinence, 'the respect we owe to our neighbour makes unseasonable in the world'. For six years all his food was fifteen figs a day at sunset, and he sometimes fasted three or four days without eating at all. He worked at cultivating his bit of ground and, in imitation of the Egyptian monks, making baskets, and he thus provided himself with the few necessaries of life. During the first dozen years he had no other shelter than a sort of arbour of reeds and rushes woven together; afterwards he built himself a cell, which was still to be seen in St Jerome's time: it was four feet broad and five in height, and a little longer than his body, and was built of mud bricks, rubble and broken tiles. When he found that figs alone were insufficient to support life properly, he allowed himself to eat vegetables, bread and oil; but advancing age was never allowed to lessen his austerities, as it did not lessen the many spiritual trials and temptations that he had to meet and overcome. St Jerome mentions that though he lived so many years in Palestine, Hilarion only once visited the holy places at Jerusalem and then stayed only one day: he went once that he might not seem to despise what the Church honours, but did not go oftener lest he should appear to believe that God or his due worship is confined to any special places.

Of the many miracles that were attributed to Hilarion the first did not take place till he had spent twenty years in his desert. A woman of Eleutheropolis (Beit Jibrin, near Hebron), long married but barren, asked him to pray that

God would bless her with fruitfulness: and before the year's end she bore a son. Later, the prefect Elpidius and his wife, on their way back from a visit to St Antony, arrived at Gaza, where their three children were taken seriously ill and were given up by the local doctors. Their mother appealed to Hilarion, who went to Gaza accordingly, and when he prayed by their bedside the children safely passed their crises and soon recovered completely. Among other miraculous happenings, St Hilarion is said to have helped a Christian citizen of Maiuma, called Italicus, who was training horses to race against those of a *duumvir* of Gaza. Italicus believed that the other man was not 'on the square', that in fact he used magic to bring about his victories. So he asked help of Hilarion, who promptly lubricated his chariot wheels with water; whereupon Italicus's horses won, and the spectators exclaimed that the *duumvir's* god had been vanquished by Christ.

Settlements of hermits were made all over Palestine, and St Hilarion used to visit them on certain days before the vintage. On one of these visits he was watching the pagans assembled at Elusa, to the south of Beersheba, for the worship of their gods: many of their sick had been cured by him, so he was well known to them and they came to ask his blessing. He received them with loving gentleness and urged them to give their worship to the one only God. His words had such effect that he was not allowed to leave them till he had traced out the ground for laying the foundations of a church, and their priest, all dressed for his office as he was, had become a catechumen.

When he was some sixty-five years old Hilarion learned (by revelation, it was said) of the death of St Antony. He had been much troubled for two years past at the number of people, especially women, who crowded to him, and he was finding responsibility for his disciples a great burden. 'I have returned to the world,' he said, 'and received my reward in this life. All Palestine looks up to me; I have even got a farm and household goods, under pretext of the brethren's needs.' So he made up his mind to leave, whereupon ten thousand people assembled to stop him.[1] He told them he would neither eat nor drink till they let him go, and was as good as his word: when they had seen him pass a week without taking anything they gave up objecting. Hilarion then chose forty monks who were able to walk without eating till after sunset, and with them he travelled south-east. On the fifth day he arrived at Pelusium, and in six days more at Babylon (Fostat or Old Cairo) in Egypt. Two days later he reached Aphroditopolis (Atfieh), where he did business with the deacon Barsanes, who hired out camels to those who wanted to visit St Antony. After travelling three more days in a waterless desert they came to St Antony's mountain near the Red Sea, where they found two monks who had been his disciples.

St Hilarion walked all over the place with them. 'Here it was,' they said, 'that he sang, here he prayed: there he worked, and there he rested when he was tired. He planted these vines and these little trees: he tilled this piece of ground with his own hands; he dug this pond to water the garden and he used this hoe for several years.' Hilarion laid himself down upon Antony's bed and kissed it with tears. On the top of the mountain (the ascent was very difficult, 'twisting like a vine'), they found two cells to which he had often retired to avoid visitors and even his own disciples; and near-by was the garden where the power of Antony had made the wild asses respect his vegetables and young trees. St Hilarion asked to see the place where he was buried. They led him aside, but it is unknown whether they showed it him or no, for St Antony had given strict orders that his grave should be hidden,

[1] It is a good round number. We may understand that there was a large crowd.

lest Pergamios, a neighbouring rich man, should carry the body off and build a church for it.

St Hilarion returned to Aphroditopolis, and thence went with two others into a neighbouring wilderness where, he declared, he began for the first time to serve Jesus Christ. It had not rained there for three years, ever since the death of St Antony in fact, and the people turned for help to Hilarion whom they looked on as Antony's successor: his prayers at once obtained a plentiful downpour. Many labourers and herdmen, too, who were stung by insects or bitten by snakes, were cured by treating their wounds with oil which he had blessed. The consequence was that here also Hilarion found himself too popular, and he departed secretly towards Alexandria, whence he turned aside to a ruined suburb where several monks lived. He left the same evening, and when the monks pressed him to stay told them that it was necessary for their security that he should go. He showed the spirit of prophecy: for that night armed men arrived there to put him to death. The explanation is this. When Julian the Apostate became emperor, the heathen of Gaza destroyed Hilarion's monastery and obtained an order to kill him in revenge for the many conversions he had made; and this party had been sent into Egypt to carry out the sentence.

The Libyan desert was Hilarion's next refuge, but a year in an oasis there convinced him that he was too well known ever to find peace and quietness in Egypt, and his mind turned to the possibility of some remote island. Though the emperor Julian was now dead, he would not return to Gaza, but took ship with one companion, Zananas, for Sicily. He offered to pay their passage with a copy of the gospels which he had written out, but the master of the vessel, seeing their whole possessions consisted in that manuscript and the clothes on their backs, would not accept it; moreover, Hilarion by his prayers had healed his sick son on board the boat. They arrived safely, and from Cape Passaro travelled twenty miles up the country and found an unfrequented place in which to settle. Every day Hilarion collected sticks from the woods, bound them into a faggot, and sent Zananas to the nearest village to exchange it for food. Meanwhile, one of Hilarion's earliest disciples at Gaza, who had accompanied him into Egypt, St Hesychius, was looking for him. Eventually he tried Greece and here, at Modon in the Peloponnesus, he heard from a Jewish peddler that a prophet had appeared in Sicily who wrought many miracles. Hesychius arrived at Passaro and, inquiring for the holy man at the first village, found that everybody knew him and where he lived.

Hilarion wanted to go into some foreign country where not even his language should be understood, and so Hesychius took him to Epidaurus in Dalmatia, near Ragusa.[1] Miracles again defeated his design of living unknown. St Jerome relates that a serpent of enormous size devoured both cattle and men, and that Hilarion induced this creature to come on to a pile of wood prepared for the purpose, and then set fire to it so that it was burnt to ashes. He also tells us that, when an earthquake happened, the sea threatened to overwhelm Epidaurus. The terrified inhabitants brought Hilarion to the shore, as it were to oppose him as a strong wall against the waves: he made three crosses in the sand, then stretched out his arms towards the sea which, rising up like a high mountain, turned back. Distracted over what he should do and whither he should go, roaming alone over the world in his imagination, Hilarion complained that though his tongue was silent yet his miracles spake. At last he again fled away

---

[1] One gets the impression that old age was telling on the saint and that there was now something pathological in his restless quest for quietness and solitude.

in the night, in a small vessel to Cyprus, where he settled at a place two miles from Paphos.

From here, after two years, Hilarion sent Hesychius to Palestine to see how the brethren prospered there and to visit his first retreat at Gaza—the thoughts of the old man were dwelling on his childhood home. On his return in the spring Hesychius found that Hilarion, again troubled by visitors, wanted to escape to yet another country, but he was able to persuade him to be content with a place of retreat deeper in the island, a pleasant spot where there were running water and fruit trees. Here at last the troubled spirit found rest; and here, about the year 371, being some eighty years of age, St Hilarion died. He was visited in his last sickness by St Epiphanius, the bishop of Salamis, from whom St Jerome got much of the information for the biography which is the principal source for what is known of Hilarion. This biography is a delightful work and, though there is a strong element of romance in it, there is no good reason to doubt its historical basis.

As of others of the Desert Fathers, examples were related of St Hilarion's shrewd sayings and searching retorts. On one occasion St Epiphanius invited him to eat some roast chicken, and Hilarion declined, because, he said, it had been his rule ever since he was a monk not to eat anything that had animal life. 'Ever since I have been a monk,' rejoined Epiphanius, 'it has been my rule never to lie down to sleep without first being sure that I am at peace with all men.' 'Your rule,' replied Hilarion, 'is better than mine.' He was often called on to exorcize evil spirits, and he declared that men's sins were responsible for the demoniac possession of dumb animals, creatures of which he was very fond; and his reference to his body, 'I'll see to it, ass, that you do not kick', is likewise reminiscent of St Francis of Assisi.

At the time of Hilarion's death St Hesychius was again

absent in Palestine, and directly he heard the news he hurried back to Cyprus lest his master's body be carried off by the people of Paphos. He found that Hilarion had left a letter bequeathing to him all that he had of the world's goods—the gospel book that the shipmaster had refused, a sackcloth shirt, a cloak with a hood. So as not to excite the suspicion of those who jealously guarded the hermitage, Hesychius allowed the impression to get around that he was going to live there still, and thus, after ten months, he was able with great difficulty and risk to remove St Hilarion's body and take it back to Palestine. It was met by crowds of people, with clergy and monks, who accompanied it to the monastery at Maiuma where it was buried. And there a few years later the faithful Hesychius went to his reward.

ST MALCHUS
Captive among the Beduin

On the twelfth day of the kalends of November (October
21) the Roman Martyrology notes that there died at
Maronia, near Antioch in Syria, St Malchus, a monk, and
for the story of this Malchus we again have to thank St
Jerome, who tells us that he had it from the lips of the man
himself. This statement is a not uncommon device among
writers of edifying fiction; and the tale of Malchus is
highly romanticized, whatever element of truth may
perhaps underlie it. It was treated in 3000 lines of verse
by a monk of Canterbury, Reginald, early in the twelfth
century, and is retold here as an unusual example of hagiographical narrative.

Malchus (whose name is Jerome's latinization of
Malik) was born at Nisibis, a great Christian centre in
Mesopotamia (now Nusaybin); he was the only son of his
parents and when he grew up they wanted him to marry
that the family might be carried on. He, however, had
already resolved to give his life wholly to the direct service
of God, so he ran away from home and joined a company
of hermits in the Syrian desert near Khalkis. Some years
later he heard of the death of his father, and he went to the
elder and told him that he wished to go home for a time in
order to comfort and look after his mother. The abbot was
unsympathetic and represented the inclination to Malchus
as a subtle temptation—he had put his hand to the plow

and the Devil was urging him to look back in order that he might never return to it. Thereupon Malchus pointed out that he was now entitled to some property which he could sell and with the proceeds enlarge the buildings of the hermits, but the abbot was an honest man who had made up his mind, and he was not going to change it for a consideration of that sort. He implored his young disciple to stay where he was, but Malchus was as persuaded of his duty as the abbot was, and since he could not get permission he started off without it.

Misfortune speedily overtook him. He had no difficulty in attaching himself to a caravan, but between Aleppo and Edessa (Urfa) it was attacked and plundered by Bedu Arabs (perhaps of the Beni Ghassan), and Malchus and a young woman were carried off by one of the marauding chiefs. They were taken to the heart of the desert beyond the Euphrates, and Malchus was set to work as a sheep and goat herd among the nomads. He was not unhappy; certainly he did not like living among heathens and the heat was considerably greater than he had been accustomed to, but 'It seemed to me that my lot was very like that of holy Jacob, and I remembered Moses, both of whom had been shepherds in the wilderness. I lived on dates and cheese and milk; I prayed endlessly in my heart; and I sang the psalms that I had learned among the monks.'

No doubt his master was pleased with Malchus—men carried off as slaves were rarely so obedient and contented —and he sought to do him a service by arranging a marriage. It is incredible to the wandering tribes of the desert that any man should choose to live alone, and the unmarried man must live as a servant in the tent of another[1] for none but women do what we should call

---

[1] See Doughty's *Arabia Deserta*, Vol. 1, pp. 321, 322. The life described by Doughty is much the same as that lived fifteen hundred years ago among the black tents.

domestic work, and much more. So Malchus was told that he must marry his fellow prisoner, and thereupon he was very alarmed: not only was he a monk and so had put marriage behind him, but he also knew that the girl was already married in her own country. It would seem, however, that she was not altogether unwilling and arrangements were made for them to live together in spite of the protests of Malchus. He even went so far as to threaten to kill himself, whereupon the girl declared (over the centuries can be heard the note of wounded *amour-propre* in her voice) that she was quite indifferent to him, and that she was prepared to live with him under a mere appearance of matrimony and so avert the anger of their master. This they did, though neither of them found the arrangement completely satisfactory. 'I loved the woman as a sister,' Malchus confided, 'but I never quite trusted her as a sister.'

One day Malchus was watching a crowd of ants at work in their heap and the thought came to him how like the sight was to that of a busy and orderly company of monks. Thereupon he became suddenly very homesick, the memory of his past happiness among the hermits was more than he could bear, and when he had driven in his flocks that evening, he went and told his companion that he had made up his mind to escape. She, too, was anxious to find her real husband again and was willing enough to adventure with Malchus, so they made their preparations with all secrecy and ran away one night, carrying food in two goatskins.

By filling these skins with air and using them as a support they were able to cross the Euphrates in safety, but on the third day they saw their master and another man of the tribe, on camels, coming up with them. They hid themselves among the rocks and undergrowth near the mouth of a cave, and the chieftain, thinking he had seen them go into the cave itself, sent his man in to fetch them out. When he did not reappear, the chief himself approached and went in, but neither did he come out again. Instead there issued from the cave a lioness with a cub in her mouth, and she leaped off among the rocks, leaving the two Arabs dead on the floor of her den. Malchus and the woman ran to the tethered camels on which their pursuers had come, quickly mounted them, and set off at a great pace.

After ten days' riding they came to a Roman station in Mesopotamia, where the officer in charge listened to their story and sent them on to Edessa. From there St Malchus made his way back to the colony of hermits by Khalkis and eventually went to end his days at Maronia, where St Jerome said he talked with him. Long did his companion seek for her husband; but she never found him, and in her sorrow and disappointment her mind turned to the friend who had shared her captivity and helped her escape; she went and settled down near him, giving her time to the service of God and her neighbour, and there she died at a great age.

ST JOHN CHRYSOSTOM
Doctor of the Church

The John whom the world was to know as Chrysostom, 'golden-mouthed', was born in the great hellenized city of Antioch in Syria about the year 347, when the Christian Church was still in the throes of passing from a persecuted minority to a privileged majority in the Roman empire. His parents were of good family, and Christian; but he was given a good education on the ancient pattern and was not baptized until he had reached manhood. For some time he was a member of a community of hermit-monks in the neighbouring mountains, and with characteristic impetuosity he overdid his self-imposed austerities, and undermined his health; so he had to return home to Antioch, where in due course he was ordained deacon and priest. For twelve years his reputation as a preacher grew and grew, he became the greatest popular preacher of his time, perhaps of all time; then, in the year 398, he was chosen to be archbishop of Constantinople. He was then about fifty years old.

Constantinople, the imperial city, New Rome, was on the way to becoming what it was to be for a thousand years, the chief city of the Eastern world and the second see in the Church. Chrysostom succeeded to the chair of an old and easy-going bishop, and the new broom at once got to work, beginning at the top of the stairs, in his own household. When he extended his reforms to the indolent clergy and flighty people of the city he soon aroused opposition. That opposition spread—upwards.

What followed is a long, complex and not always clear story. It is enough to say here that Chrysostom's fierce attacks on misuse of wealth and other wickedness antagonized many of the rich and powerful, and he incurred the enmity of the empress, Eudoxia (he is said to have called her Jezebel: if he did, it was tactless, but not altogether undeserved). All this might have blown over had not the situation been manipulated from outside, by a strange, able and powerful personality, Archbishop Theophilus of Alexandria. He had personal, theological and ecclesiastico-political axes to grind, and he gathered a strong following of Egyptian and Syrian bishops to oppose the new archbishop of Constantinople.

The upshot was that, in the summer of the year 403, a gathering of bishops under Theophilus of Alexandria professed to deprive Chrysostom of his see. The emperor, Arcadius, was not a strong character (Edward Gibbon calls him a sheep, using 52 words to say it), and Chrysostom was at once sent into exile. He was scarcely gone when he was recalled: the whole circumstances are not certain, but the fact that Chrysostom was now the beloved of the city mob had something to do with it, for the emperor feared the mob. Chrysostom, indeed, has sometimes been accused of being a demagogue; in fact he was not, but on occasion his enthusiasm betrayed him into talking like one.

However, there was only a temporary respite for him. The empress Eudoxia soon had another grievance against him; Theophilus again pulled wires (but without venturing to revisit Constantinople, where the people had threatened to throw him into the sea): and, twelve months after the first exile, Chrysostom was again banished. He was taken to Cucusus in the Taurus mountains, on the borders of Armenia. He did not come back alive.

As well as over 700 of his sermons and some other writings, a large number of Chrysostom's letters written from exile have been preserved; and very precious they are. They show him at his best. As a bishop: concerned for the confusion in his church and for those who suffered under the persecution that was meted out to those who supported him; giving directions, too, for the carrying on of missionary and other enterprises he had undertaken. As a friend: so affectionate, so considerate for others, so solicitous for the religious and temporal welfare of his correspondents; rebuking, sternly or gently, especially those who had failed to write to him; praising lavishly, especially those who were patient and faithful to him. As a man: recounting his sufferings from ill-health (one suspects he was a 'bad patient'), from the rigours of the climate and from raids by the Isaurians.

But it was this letter-writing, together with the number of people who contrived to visit him and get encouragement and instructions, that was Chrysostom's undoing. He was keeping his cause alive throughout the East; as even Gibbon recognizes, 'every tongue repeated the praises of his genius and virtue, and the respectful attention of the Christian world was fixed on a desert spot among the mountains of Taurus'. This did not suit the authorities at Constantinople, and after three years orders came for his removal to a far more remote spot, at the eastern end of the Black Sea. Prematurely aged, Chrysostom set out on the long journey in charge of two soldiers. At the end of some weeks of travelling amid the heats and rains of high summer, he was taken ill near Comana in Pontus, and in a few hours he was dead. We are told that his last words on earth were: 'Glory to God for all things. Amen.' It was September 14 in the year 407.

'Great is the office of a bishop,' Chrysostom had said, 'for Christ teaches us that we must lay down our lives for the sheep; we must never desert them, but stand up against the wolves. The shepherd differs from the hireling. . . When men would kill Christ, he neither altered his gospel nor betrayed those who trusted in him: like the good shepherd, he stood firm, and died.'

It was not till the eve of his final banishment that Chrysostom and others concerned had appealed to the pope, St Innocent I. Innocent was nonplussed at what had happened: he wrote kindly to Chrysostom, severely to Theophilus of Alexandria. With other Italian bishops he induced the Western emperor, Honorius, to write to his Eastern brother, Arcadius, to co-operate in convening a council to examine the matter: but the delegation of bishops carrying the letter was prevented by force from delivering it to Arcadius. The council was never summoned—the difficulties were too great. Pope Innocent refused to recognize Chrysostom's intruded successor at Constantinople, and broke off communion with Theophilus of Alexandria and all who supported them: that was all he could do. It must almost have looked as if the personal injustice to Chrysostom, and all the canonical irregularities involved, had gone by default. It was ten years before amends were made in Constantinople and communion with Old Rome restored: meanwhile, as was said, 'the voices of John's friends were raised in blessing on his memory—but God alone heard them'.

Of Chrysostom's actual life, apart from the 'high lights' not a great deal is known; on the other hand, much can be gleaned about him personally from his sermons and writings. Like many of us, he tended to mellow as he got older—but not by any means in all respects. It is clear that he could never stomach Eudoxia; she was an imperial example of a type that any parish priest today would recognize at sight. Much more important, he never ceased to be an outspoken fighter for what is now called 'social justice': there was no modification of his castigating of ill-gotten wealth and the unjust rich, nor of his passionate pleas for generous alms-giving, according to their means by the poor as well as by the comfortably-off. Chrysostom's *sympathy* in this and similar matters must be emphasized. He denounced sin as sin; but at the same time he felt from his heart for its victims, both for the victims of their own sins and the victims of the sins of others. He indeed had compassion on the multitude. He was moved no less by the unhappiness of the poor or oppressed than by the guiltiness of the sinner. He never gives the impression that, in his concern for the observance of divine law, he was unmoved by the sufferings of the human spirit.

Some people have tried to fix the label 'puritan' on Chrysostom, because of his repeated and unsparing denunciations of the public games and shows, and of the faithful who flocked to them. In fact, those denunciations were amply justified, on moral, social, economic and even political grounds: over and above that, there was still a living memory—though Chrysostom does not seem directly to refer to it—of the association of those spectacles with idolatrous worship—those mysterious 'pomps' that we renounce at baptism.

John's friendliness and informality come out in many of his sermons, whether he is talking about the highest Christian mysteries, or about the bossiness of husbands, or about the cruelty of some wives. He, as much as any medieval friar (though differently), was a 'people's preacher': he speaks in plain language and makes clear at every turn that he is intimately acquainted with the daily life and joys and temptations and sufferings of his people; he threatens, he sympathizes, he caricatures, and he has the art of making the unexpected point. When commenting on St Paul's advice to Timothy (Chrysostom knew St Paul by heart), the advice to 'take a little wine', he begins: 'Paul did not say simply "take wine" but "a little wine"; and this not because Timothy stood in need of that advice —but because we do.'

A good deal of information can be found in Chrysostom's sermons about contemporary customs of worship, the place of the eucharistic assembly in Christian life, and the abuses that were prevalent; and it is interesting to notice his emphasis on the teaching function of the liturgy and on the supremacy of corporate public prayer. At the same time he urges the necessity of private prayer, which, he says again and again, must be a raising of the heart and mind to God and not simply 'asking for something', though petition is good. The grace of the Holy Spirit makes every good Christian a temple of God's worship; daily work can be done prayerfully, and some occupations leave the mind free for direct prayer: 'It does not matter,' he repeats, 'where or when it is, provided you pray sincerely. . . Only one thing matters to God: a religious heart, integrity of soul.' But public worship comes first, and he meets an objection that is still heard: 'Certainly you can pray at home: but not so well as at church, joined with the company of the faithful. There the cry of the worshippers goes up with one voice, and the presiding clergy unite the weaker and the stronger supplications into one great prayer to Heaven.'

In spite of the touches of Greek subtlety, and a famous and much-discussed incident[1] that wrung a cry of protest from his English biographer, Dean Stephens, Chrysostom was doggedly honest and outspoken. Honest with a bluntness that made him many enemies: how much of his

---

[1] The making bishop of his friend Basil (not the saint). See W. R. W. Stephens, *Saint John Chrysostom, his Life and Times* (1883), pp. 40-43, and D. Attwater, *St John Chrysostom* (1959), pp. 26-27.

troubles he brought on himself by his forthrightness and lack of tact cannot now be known—but the evidence suggests it was not a little. Yet with all his righteous indignation—that dangerous thing—one is never in doubt with Chrysostom that he loved, really loved, those whom he chastened. He was, as might be said nowadays, a 'Bible Christian', and one of the greatest of all interpreters of the Scriptures. And, characteristically, he was opposed to their allegorical interpretation whenever a literal, historical meaning was possible. His enormous preaching output was in the main devoted to expounding the Bible so that his hearers—ordinary people—might know and understand the apostolic tradition and its practical application. He was a great practical moralist, and could draw a moral from anything. 'You praise my words,' he exclaimed over and over again, 'and greet my exhortations with loud applause. But show you approval by obedience—that is the praise I want, the applause of your good deeds.' St John Chrysostom was a priest and a bishop, a man of action, a shepherd of souls and bodies, whose business it was to live the Christian religion and to help his flock to do the same; and he was impatient of whatever seemed to be a hindrance to that work, especially when that hindrance came from wealthy and privileged people who were oppressing and corrupting the poor, the weak and the friendless. Surely these are things that speak strongly to the condition of very many English-speaking Christians today.

And then there is what we nowadays call his personality. It has been summed up by John Henry Newman himself, who wrote: 'I consider St Chrysostom's charm to lie in his intimate sympathy and compassionateness for the whole world, not only in its strength but in its weakness: in the lively regard with which he views everything that comes before him, taken in the concrete. . ., the interest which he takes in all things, not so far as God has made them all alike, but as he has made them different from each other. I speak of his versatile recognition of men, one by one, for the sake of that portion of good, be it more or less, of a lower order or a higher, which has been severally lodged in them. . . He may indeed be said in some sense to have a devotion of his own for every one who comes across him— for persons, ranks, classes, callings, societies, considered as divine works and the subjects of his good offices or good will. . . It is this observant benevolence which gives to his exposition of Scripture its chief characteristic.' As well as something about Chrysostom, that passage tells us something about Newman.

In the East St John Chrysostom's principal feast-day is November 13, but in the West it is January 27. It was on this day in the year 438 that his body was laid in the church of the Apostles at Constantinople, having been brought from Comana by order of the emperor Theodosius II and St Pulcheria, the children of Arcadius and Eudoxia.

ST PULCHERIA
Empress

Among the women of the Byzantine Roman empire who took a decisive part in public affairs or were distinguished for intellectual achievement were the two Theodoras, wives respectively of the emperors Justinian and Theophilus, Irene, widow of Leo IV, Anna Comnena, daughter of Alexius I (the historian of her father's reign), and in the fourteenth century, and of lower social rank, another Irene, whose conversation reminded her hearers of Plato and Pythagoras—or so they said. These are well known and their names often occur; but less attention is commonly given to a princess who has been accorded the honours of sainthood with a good deal more reason than some other distinguished Byzantine ladies—the *augusta* Pulcheria.

In the year 408 the emperor Arcadius died and was succeeded by his son Theodosius II, a boy of seven. For six years affairs were capably directed by the praetorian prefect, and then he probably died, for in 414 the princess Pulcheria, sister of the emperor, was proclaimed *augusta* and, though only fifteen years of age, two years older than Theodosius, she became active regent for and guardian of her brother. She had been an orphan since she was nine, but her upbringing had been in consonance with her natural qualities, and her intelligence, virtue and administrative ability were already mature: what she lacked in experience she made up in wisdom and quickness of apprehension. Theodosius was quite different: he was good and well-meaning but too gentle for public life; he was less interested in the arts of government and diplomacy than in natural science and hunting, and especially painting and handwriting, so that he was nicknamed 'the Calligrapher'.

Under Pulcheria's control the court was a striking contrast with what it had been in the days of her mother Eudoxia, who had incurred the wrath of St John Chrysostom (cf. page 60). On becoming *augusta*, Pulcheria made a vow of virginity and induced her two sisters to do the same. There can be no doubt that her motive for doing this was not wholly, perhaps not even primarily, religious: she was a realistic young woman of affairs, and did not want her political administration upset and perhaps her brother to lose his throne through the aspirations of ambitious men to marry her or the princesses her sisters. But neither was the vow devoid of religion; she had called on God to be her witness and she did not take his name in vain: she kept her vow, even after she was in fact married. But to represent the court at this time as a sort of monastery is an exaggeration: the spectacle of the young princesses spending much time spinning and embroidering and in church was nothing out of the ordinary, and if Pulcheria forbade men access to her own and her sisters' apartments that was a measure of elementary prudence—tongues will always wag and Byzantine court officials were not consistently well behaved. We get the impression of a united and busy family, of which the main domestic concern was the education and training of the young Theodosius. Pulcheria herself was a fluent speaker and writer of both Latin and Greek, and a ready use of those two tongues was to be as much a part of her brother's equipment as horsemanship and the use of arms; he had, too, to learn to carry himself well in public at civil and ecclesiastical ceremonies, to understand the Christian religion, and sincerely to practise it. Unfortunately, like so many more than ordinarily capable people, Pulcheria was too self-sufficient, and she (perhaps unconsciously at first) took advantage of her brother's lack of enthusiasm for public affairs; the result was that he grew up virtuous and scholarly, but no ruler. As George Finlay caustically puts it, 'His incapacity for business was so great that he is hardly accused of having augmented the misfortunes of his reign by his own acts'— or the predominant good fortunes either—which can mostly be put down to St Pulcheria. Both her thoroughness and her brother's indifference are illustrated by the story that on one occasion, in order to test him, Pulcheria drew up and presented to him a decree containing a sentence of death against herself. He signed it without reading it.

When the time came for Theodosius to marry, Pulcheria had again in view the avoidance of political complications and, it must be admitted, the safeguarding of her own ascendancy, which certainly in the circumstances was for the good of the state. Her choice fell on Athenais, the beautiful and highly accomplished daughter of an Athenian philosopher named Leontios, who was still a pagan.[1] She was acceptable to Theodosius and had no objection to becoming a Christian, so in 421 they were married. The emperor was then twenty and Athenais, or Eudokia as she had been christened, twenty-seven. It was in the years following this marriage that two of the principal achievements of St Pulcheria and Theodosius were carried out. The one was the foundation (or reorganization) in 425 of the 'university' of Constantinople, in opposition to the school of Athens; it had numerous professors of Greek as

[1] The story of Athenais being sent to Constantinople to seek her fortune throws an interesting sidelight on Greek society at this period. For a summary, see Finlay's *Greece Under the Romans*, cap. ii, sect. 11.

well as of Latin grammar and rhetoric, which for the first time gave the Greek language an official position in the Eastern empire apart from its use in church services. Theodosius and Pulcheria were, in fact, the first rulers of Constantinople who were Greek rather than Latin in mind and inclination: especially was this true of the emperor, but for whose ineffectiveness of character the change would have been more clearly marked. The other achievement was the drawing up and publication of a code of law: Pulcheria had gauged the need of rulers and people for fixed principles of law to which either could appeal, and this need was met by the Code of Theodosius. Later, their reign was marked by two remissions of arrears of taxes, in 414 for forty years up to 408 and in 443 for twenty years up to 428 (I am sorry if this statement shocks any reader who is concerned in fiscal administration; but in those days not only could taxes be forty years overdue but rulers would sometimes remit them in the interests of their subjects).

St Pulcheria corresponded with St Cyril of Alexandria about the heresy of Nestorius, condemned at the Council of Ephesus in 431, and with Pope St Leo the Great about Eutyches and the monophysite heresy, rejected by the Council of Chalcedon in 451; clergy from all over the empire appealed to her when in difficulties. She was responsible for the building of a number of churches, one of which in Constantinople was to house the *Hodegetria*, a famous *eikon* of our Lady which had been sent from Jerusalem, its painting being attributed (falsely) to St Luke the Evangelist. In one small matter Pulcheria left her mark on the Western church. She had the body of St John Chrysostom brought back to Constantinople, and in 438 it was enshrined in the church of the Apostles: this was on January 27, and on the anniversary of that translation Chrysostom's feast is observed in the Latin rite, instead of on the day of his death. Such was Pulcheria's zeal for orthodoxy that the conciliar fathers at Chalcedon hailed her as 'Guardian of the faith, peacemaker, religious right-believer, a second Saint Helen'.

It was inevitable that the *augusta* Eudokia should sooner or later attempt to undermine the influence of her sister-in-law, and the first open breach came after the condemnation of Nestorianism. Cyril of Alexandria had written on behalf of orthodoxy both to Pulcheria and Eudokia, and Pulcheria had persuaded Theodosius to accept the condemnation. Thus far Pulcheria had held her own; but Eudokia was indignant at her husband's lack of determination and stirred up the lower elements among the Nestorians to spread gross slanders about the emperor's sister. Theodosius was eventually so worked on as to order the patriarch of Constantinople, St Flavian, to make Pulcheria a deaconess of his church and so withdraw her from the court. Flavian objected, but Theodosius, egged on by Eudokia, was firm for once, and there was nothing for the patriarch to do but feign obedience; but first he sent a message to Pulcheria warning her to keep out of the way. She took the hint and retired to her country house at Hebdomon.

St Pulcheria's exile lasted for some years. We may well believe that she 'looked upon her retreat as a favour of Heaven and consecrated all her time to God in prayer and good works. She made no complaint of her brother's ingratitude, of the empress who owed everything to her, or of their unjust ministers' (Alban Butler). And no doubt she would have been glad 'both to forget the world and to be forgotten by it' but for the fact that she had responsibilities in respect of that great part of the world whose metropolis was at Constantinople. For a time things went fairly well, but about the year 441 came the fall of Eudokia. She was accused, probably unjustly, of infidelity with a handsome but gouty officer named Paulinus[1]; he was beheaded and Eudokia was exiled to Jerusalem, under guise of a pilgrimage. She never came back. There was a general shuffling of offices at court, and Pulcheria was recalled, but not to her old position of control, which was now held by Khrysaphios, an old supporter of Eudokia. Under his administration the Eastern part of the empire went from bad to worse for ten years.

Under pressure from this man, and with a fine disregard for theological consistency seeing that he had formerly favoured Nestorius, Theodosius gave support to the monophysites. In 449 Pope St Leo appealed to St Pulcheria and to the emperor to reject Monophysism; the answer of Theodosius was to approve the acts of the 'Robber Synod' of Ephesus and to drive St Flavian from the see of Constantinople. Pulcheria was firmly orthodox, but her influence over her brother was no longer strong enough to control him. The pope wrote again, and the archdeacon of Rome, Hilarus, wrote, and so did the Western emperor Valentinian III and Eudoxia, his wife (Theodosius's daughter), and Galla Placidia, his mother—and amid all these appeals Theodosius II suddenly died, killed by a fall from his horse while hunting.

St Pulcheria, now fifty-one years old, at once became mistress of the Eastern empire. The nomination of a new emperor was left to her, and she selected Marcian, a middle-aged soldier from Thrace of the highest reputation. This choice was due to Aspar, the powerful general whose chief of staff Marcian had been. The new emperor was crowned by Pulcheria in the presence of the senate on 24 August 450. To secure his title to the empire she offered herself to him in marriage on condition that her vow of

---

[1] For the fantastic story of the Phrygian apple see Finlay, *loc. cit.* Gibbon says of it that it is a story 'fit only for the *Arabian Nights*, where something not very unlike it can be found'.

virginity should be respected; Marcian agreed, and the marriage took place.

The joint reign was a happy one, both in internal affairs and external relations. It began with the execution of Khrysaphios as an enemy of the state, which was quickly followed by a prohibition of the sale of offices—though whether this salutary law was strictly enforced is another matter. Four legates were received from Pope Leo, and under the imperial protection the Council of Chalcedon was convened in 451 and Monophysism condemned; Pulcheria and Marcian attended its sixth session in person, and in writing to thank them Leo declared that it was largely through Pulcheria's own efforts that truth had been vindicated against the errors both of Nestorius and the monophysites. They did their best to get the decrees of Chalcedon accepted over all the East, but failed lamentably in Egypt and Syria, where Monophysism is professed (at any rate in theory) by many Christians to this day; St Pulcheria herself wrote two letters, one to certain monks, the other to an abbess of nuns in Palestine, pointing out how the council had not (as was averred) revived Nestorianism, but had condemned that heresy together with the opposed errors of Eutyches. It has already been mentioned that Pulcheria had prompted two remissions of unpaid taxes under Theodosius, and she and her husband inaugurated a policy of low taxation and as little warfare as possible; Marcian, it has been said, 'was a soldier who loved peace without fearing war', and one of his first acts was to refuse payment of the tribute which Attila the Hun had been wont to exact from Theodosius. The war which threatened in consequence was averted by Attila's death.

The spirit in which these sovereigns undertook their duties was expressed by Marcian in his declaration that 'It is our business to provide for the care of the human race,' and how well they succeeded in the eyes of their subjects was shown forty years later when the citizens greeted Anastasius I with a shout of 'Govern like Marcian!' But this excellent partnership lasted for only three years; in July of the year 453 the empress Pulcheria died. She bequeathed all her huge private fortune for religious and charitable purposes, and her directions in this regard were faithfully carried out.

The feast of St Pulcheria, Virgin, Empress of Constantinople, New Rome, is observed in very many Byzantine churches, and towards the end of the sixteenth century Cardinal Baronius added her name to the Roman Martyrology on September 10—a happier and more worthy addition than some of the others that we owe to that venerable and learned scholar.

In another class of appreciation there may be quoted the approval of Edward Gibbon—and he was a man not easily pleased: 'She alone, among all the descendants of the great Theodosius [I], appears to have inherited any share of his manly spirit and abilities. . . Her deliberations were maturely weighed; her actions were prompt and decisive: and, while she moved without noise or ostentation the wheel of government, she discreetly attributed to the genius of the emperor the long tranquillity of his reign . . . Theodosius the Younger was never reduced to the disgraceful necessity of encountering and punishing a rebellious subject: and since we cannot applaud the vigour, some praise may be due to the mildness and prosperity of the administration of Pulcheria' (*Decline and Fall of the Roman Empire*, cap. xxxii).

ST JOHN THE ALMSGIVER
Patriarch of Alexandria

This John was the son of one Epiphanius who was governor of Cyprus during the middle years of the sixth century, and he was born at Amathus (near Limassol) in that island. He was given an education suitable to his rank, and in due course he settled down, married, and had a number of children. Nothing is known of his career for the greater part of his life; but it is likely that these years were spent in public affairs: a contemporary says of him that 'he was always friendly to everybody, giving help, advice and encouragement, reconciling adversaries, doing kindnesses, and manifesting his love for virtue in every way', which seems to imply that he was in the public eye.

At times unknown, John was deprived by death of his wife and all his children, but it was not till he was some fifty years old, about the year 610, that he appears as a churchman. On the death of the patriarch of Alexandria, Theodore the Writer, the emperor Heraclius chose John to succeed to the see; this was on the advice of the patrician Nicetas, who was a relative of John's, and with the approval of the Alexandrian citizens. This last circumstance suggests that either John was very well known, or else that he was already living in Alexandria. The fact that he was still a layman was less surprising then than it would be now; but John's biographer does remark that 'although he had never been a monk or spent his time in church with the clergy . . . he so mastered ecclesiastical administration and attained such personal holiness that he excelled many who had been great ascetics in the desert'.

At this time the Church in Egypt had been ravaged by the monophysite heresy, and orthodox Christians were already in a minority there. We are told that when John came to the chair of Alexandria there were only seven orthodox churches in the city; but by his death he had increased them ten-fold. Such achievements as this were not brought about by the violence and chicanery which had been such a characteristic of ecclesiastical politics in Egypt; the new patriarch chose a better way, the way which earned him the people's respect and love, and the name of 'Almsgiver'.

When St John took possession of his see, he at once gave orders that a list should be drawn up of 'all my masters, down to the least of them'. When asked what he meant by that, he replied, 'The people whom you call poor and beggars are my masters and helpers, for it is only they who can really help us and bring us to the kingdom of Heaven.' The names came to over 7000 in number, and to each one he allotted a daily allowance of money. At the same time he issued a decree regulating weights and measures in the markets, with penalties for those who should transgress. A benefaction of John's that is specially mentioned was the building and endowment of seven lying-in hospitals in the city; each had forty beds, and the women stayed there a week after confinement, each one receiving a 'maternity benefit' on leaving. In addition he built a number of homes for the aged and infirm, and also hospices for travellers; nor did he hesitate to tax the clergy of the whole patriarchate for the benefit of their poorer members.

When the Persians invaded Syria and sacked Jerusalem

in 614, refugees came flocking into Egypt, and for them St John provided. Not content with that, he sent large amounts of money, food and materials to Jerusalem, as well as a special sum to ransom hundreds of nuns who had been captured by the invaders. In an accompanying letter to the patriarchal *locum tenens* there, he wrote: 'I assure you that were it possible I would myself come and work at the holy place where Christ our God rose from the dead. But do not, I pray you, reverend Sir, inscribe my unworthy name anywhere: rather, beseech Christ that it may be written in the book that is truly blessed.'

St John kept in constant close touch with his people. Twice a week he sat outside his cathedral with one or two officials, to settle disagreements and see justice done for all comers. When he found that some of the faithful were in the habit of leaving the church during divine service to chatter with their friends outside, he too went out and joined the throng. Seeing the raised eyebrows around him, he observed quietly, 'My children, the shepherd must be with his flock.' The implied rebuke was enough. Once he was leaving a church at Canopus when a woman came up, clamouring that her differences with her son-in-law should be remedied. The patriarch's attendants tried to hustle her away, telling her to come another time; but he stopped them, saying, 'How can I expect God to listen to my prayers if I do not listen to what this woman wants? To-morrow may be too late, I may be dead.'

The patrician Nicetas complained that the patriarch was misusing money in his lavish charities, money that ought to go into the impoverished imperial treasury, but John won him over to another view. And he himself set an example of frugal living: when, for instance, he visited the shrine of St Menas and was offered a cup of expensive foreign wine, he refused it: 'I do not deserve such excellent wine as that,' he said, 'which is very expensive too. Give me some local wine: its taste is nothing to boast of, but it costs less.' A wealthy layman brought him a good blanket for his modest bed, and John sold it and bought several less costly ones for his 'masters'. This happened three times running: 'We shall see whether you or I get tired of this first!' he remarked. John enjoyed getting money out of the wealthy, and used to say that 'if in order to help the needy one is able, without ill-will, to strip the rich down to their shirts, one is not doing wrong, especially if they are heartless skinflints'; and he would quote the tale of St Epiphanius of Salamis purloining money from another bishop and giving it to those in want.

Page after page of St John's Life is filled with stories, circumstantial and convincing for the most part, illustrative of his character and especially of his endless almsdeeds and passion for 'social justice'. Not the least interesting to an English reader is the account of a certain 'foreign sea-captain who had fallen on hard times'. John gave him money, which helped him to buy a cargo of goods, but his ship came to grief immediately on clearing the harbour at Alexandria. John rebuked the man for mixing money given in kindness with money from a bad source, and doubled his former gift. The captain was again wrecked, and this time lost his ship as well as his merchandise. Again the patriarch came to the rescue, providing a ship and 20,000 bushels of corn. The captain sailed westward, and after three weeks ran into a heavy gale and found himself off the coast of the island of Britain (doubtless, from what follows, Cornwall). On landing, they found the people in the grip of famine, and soon bartered their corn for cash and a load of tin. They departed rejoicing, and subsequently rejoiced still more: for their cargo of tin was found to contain silver as well. 'He who multiplied the five loaves and turned the Nile waters into blood . . . easily wrought this miracle too, in order to enrich his servant [the patriarch] and show mercy to the captain.'[1]

When the Persian forces threatened Alexandria in 619, St John decided to retire to his native Cyprus, and Nicetas prevailed on him first to visit the emperor at Constantinople, 'the queen of cities'. But on the way, at Rhodes, John had what seemed a clear intimation from Heaven that the end of his earthly journey was at hand. 'You asked me to go to our king here below,' he said to Nicetas, 'but the King above has anticipated you: he has summoned my unworthy self to him.' So he went directly to his Cypriot birthplace, Amathus, and there dictated his last will and testament. In it he said that when he was put at the head of the Alexandrian church there were 8000 pounds of gold in its treasury, and the further sums he received from Christ-loving people were very large indeed: 'I considered the matter and realized that this money belonged to the Lord of all things, and so I did my best to render to God the things that were God's. Now I have but one coin left: that, too, is God's, and I direct that it be given to those who are God's.'

St John the Almsgiver died in 619, on November 11, on which day he is honoured by the Greeks and Cypriots; but the Roman Martyrology names him on January 23, the anniversary of the translation of his relics to Constantinople. He was the original patron saint of the Knights Hospitallers, now known as the Order of St John of Jerusalem (or 'of Malta').

---

[1] John's predecessor but one at Alexandria, Eulogius, also had a link with England. St Gregory the Great wrote to him about the progress of the mission he had sent to evangelize the heathen Anglo-Saxons, a mission in which Eulogius seems to have had a personal interest.

ST MAXIMUS THE CONFESSOR
Abbot

From the middle of the fifth century the Church in the East was convulsed by the teaching of what came to be called Monophysism. According to this doctrine there is only one nature in the person of Jesus Christ, his manhood being absorbed in his divinity, which seems logically to involve the denial that our incarnate Lord is a real man. To it was opposed the doctrine defined as true by the Council of Chalcedon in the year 451, that in the person of Christ are two natures, divine and human, each keeping its own proper character. As a result of various factors, many Eastern Christians rejected the council's decision, and eventually formed the monophysite churches which exist, in a reduced form, to this day.[1]

In the era that followed the Council of Chalcedon many attempts were made to reconcile the monophysites, not only by the ecclesiastical authorities but also by the emperors at Constantinople, whose secular responsibilities were gravely embarrassed by the people's religious divisions. It was the emperor Heraclius (d. 641) who, in concert with the patriarch Sergius of Constantinople, pro-

[1] Namely, those of the Copts in Egypt, the Ethiopians, the Jacobite Syrians, the Armenians and, centuries later, the Jacobites in India. With the small remnant of Nestorians in Iraq, these Christians are out of communion with both Catholics and Orthodox, and have been in a state of separation continuously for 1500 years.

duced successive formulas designed to conciliate the dissidents. But they met with wide objection from the orthodox, being condemned as heretical by the patriarch of Jerusalem, St Sophronius, and, after Pope Honorius I had 'hedged', by his three successors in the papal chair. The rejected doctrine, known as Monothelism, affirmed that in Christ there is one single will and one operation (or energy), and not the 'two natural wills . . . the human will following and subject to the divine' as orthodox teaching demands. It was during the disturbances that followed the appearance of Monothelism that St Maximus the Confessor came into the public eye. His opposition to the heresy is by no means the only thing for which he is remembered, but his external activities in this matter and their results for himself are the principal events of his life of which records have survived.

Maximus belonged to a family of the Byzantine nobility and was born in Constantinople about the year 580. We are told that during his education he already drew attention to himself by his devotedness to philosophical and theological studies, but the first event in his life that we hear of was when he was appointed chief secretary to the emperor, Heraclius. After a time he resigned this post, and received the monastic habit in the monastery of Chrysopolis, opposite Constantinople across the Bosporus; he was soon made abbot of the community, an office he discharged well, 'indulging neither himself nor others'. His leaving the confidence and court of the unorthodox emperor calls to mind the similar step in analogous circumstances of two men in distant England and distant ages, Thomas à Becket and Thomas More; and for him as for them the ultimate upshot was martyrdom. It is true that Maximus was not a martyr in the strictest sense; but his death was a direct result of the brutal treatment meted out to him when an old man in punishment for his faithful-

ness to the integrity of the Christian faith, and the epithet
martyr is often accorded him.

But Maximus had not been many years at Chrysopolis
when he had to flee before the advancing Persians. In 632
he was at Alexandria, and it was then that his 'master,
father and teacher', as he calls him, was St Sophronius of
Jerusalem, who had been a hermit and monk in Egypt and
Palestine. Sophronius was also the outstanding opponent
of Monothelism, and when he died shortly after the capture
of Jerusalem by the Saracens in 637, Maximus, who had
already been active against Monophysism, continued his
teacher's work with great energy. He supported Pope John
IV's defence of the orthodoxy of Pope Honorius, which
had been impugned; and at a public debate in North
Africa, at Carthage, he persuaded the monothelite
patriarch of Constantinople, Pyrrhus, of his error. Some
years before, Maximus had written regarding Pyrrhus:
'Before all else, let him be quick to satisfy the Roman see,
for then all will agree that he is godly and orthodox. A man
speaks in vain . . . who does not satisfy the blessed pope of
the holy church of the Romans, that is, the apostolic see
which has received universal and supreme dominion,
authority and power of binding and loosing over all God's
holy churches everywhere from the incarnate Son of God
himself, as recognized by the holy councils. . .' So to
Rome Pyrrhus went from Africa, and made his abjuration
before Pope Theodore I; but later on he relapsed into
misbelief.

The emperor Constans II tried to end the monothelite
controversy by a decree, called the Typos, which forbade
the continuance of the dispute and ordered both sides to
keep silence about it. But the Church cannot remain silent
when challenged by falsehood, and St Maximus urged the
pope, St Martin I, to summon a council to deal with this
development, and took a prominent part in it when it met

at the Lateran in 649. The fathers of the council again condemned Monothelism, and rejected 'the vicious Typos'. The emperor was infuriated by this defiance, and by Pope Martin's continued opposition to his will; eventually he had Martin brought by force to Constantinople, where he was treated with much indignity and cruelty and exiled to the Crimea. He survived there only a few months, dying from the hardships to which he had been subjected—the last martyr pope so far in the Church's history.

It was probably some little time after the arrest of Pope Martin that St Maximus also was seized in Rome and carried off to Constantinople. He was now an old man of seventy-five, and there was no more freedom for him. He was taken off the ship at Constantinople by men who roughly and disrespectfully led him away to prison. The charge against him was that he had, by his inveterate opposition to the imperial Typos, brought harm to the empire, and after a few days he was subjected to several examinations. He made his position quite clear: when asked why he had condemned the church of Constantinople, he replied: 'I condemn no one. But I would rather lose my life than depart from the smallest point of Christian faith.' It was accordingly reported to Constans that Maximus continued in his obstinacy, and the emperor ordered that he should be taken into exile at Bizya in Thrace.

Here a bishop, Theodosius, was sent to reason with him, and finding Maximus suffering from cold and neglect he gave him money and a gown; but as soon as the visitor had departed the garment was confiscated by the local bishop. Shortly afterwards Maximus was sent, now with every mark of respect, to a neighbouring monastery, where Bishop Theodosius again visited him, together with two patricians. This time Maximus was promised honours and the imperial favour if he would accept the Typos, and once more he refused, whereupon the patricians lost their temper; they heaped abuse and insults on the old monk, and even attacked him physically, so that Theodosius had to intervene and drag them away. The next day an official arrived, who proceeded to strip Maximus of his monastic dress and to read the emperor's decision: 'Since you do not want honours, you shall be deprived of those you already have. You shall share the lot of your two followers.' This referred to Maximus's faithful disciple Anastasius and a papal commissioner (*apocrisiarius*), also named Anastasius, who were already in detention at Perbera on the western shore of the sea of Marmara.

St Maximus was taken to the same place, and his confinement there lasted six years, during which the monothelite controversy dragged on (it did not finally come to an end till 680, when the sixth general council of the Church, the third at Constantinople, again condemned the heresy). In 662 the three confessors were taken back to the capital and brought before a council of prelates, supporters of the emperor, by whom their condemnation was inevitable. With them, the memory of Pope Martin and Sophronius of Jerusalem was anathematized as well. At the emperor's bidding they were sentenced to be severely flogged, to have their tongues cut out and to be imprisoned for life in distant parts.

The ferocious sentence was carried out, St Maximus suffering the further barbarity of having his right hand chopped off. Tongueless, he could no longer preach the orthodox faith, handless, he could no longer write it; but he could still confess it by suffering with patience and dying with fortitude. He was removed after a cruel journey to Skhemaris, at the southern end of the Black Sea, and we are told that soon after arriving there he foresaw the day of his impending death in a vision. And it happened accordingly, on 13 August 662; he was eighty-two years old. Local tradition declared that for long afterwards the burial-place of Maximus was marked by supernatural light at night time.

The monk Anastasius died a short time before his master, during or at the end of the journey to his place of imprisonment. Anastasius the Apocrisiary survived in a fortress of the Caucasus until 666; it is through a letter of his that the few particulars of the last days of these confessors are known. He relates that they were shamefully treated, their captors even taking away every little thing that kind friends had given them, down to supplies of needles and thread. The two SS Anastasius are named with St Maximus in the Roman Martyrology on August 13; his feast in the Greek calendar is on January 21.

St Maximus the Confessor was an important writer on a variety of religious subjects, and a difficult one, on account both of his high themes and his laboured and obscure style. He has always been held in great honour as a theologian in the Greek-speaking East, especially as a mystical theologian, and it is in that capacity that he has lately aroused considerable interest in the West, where he has hitherto been little known, though he had already attracted attention here in the ninth century. It has now, indeed, been claimed for him that he was the father of Byzantine mysticism in its fullest sense; but this in fact originated with the desert monks of the fourth century, and Maximus may more reasonably be called its best expounder and the master of many ascetics who followed him. The aim and object of Christian life is union with God, of whose promises we are the heirs, made 'sharers in the divine nature', as it were deified by God the Son taking our flesh. By charity man's will is made one with God's will; by prayer, persevering effort and loving contemplation the Christian follows his Saviour, who submitted his human will completely to the divine will. There is the link between Maximus's own inner life and the seemingly obscure theological doctrine for which he contended so resolutely and suffered so much, two things whose relationship to one another may not be immediately obvious. The divine incarnation, God's union with man, enables man to be restored in the image of God, which was spoiled by the sin of our first parents; and the union with God of man thus deified is maintained by charity: there resides the heart of Maximus's teaching.

One of his outstanding works is the *Mystagogy*, wherein he studies the 'symbolical actions carried out in the liturgical rites of the holy Church'; but the one having an appeal for the general reader, available in English,[1] is the *Four Centuries on Love* (agape), each consisting of one hundred paragraphs, ranging from two or three to a score of lines. The English translators are surely right in calling this 'one of the most profound and beautiful works in all Christian writing'. The author himself says that 'Many people will find that much of it will need careful enquiry, although at the first glance it may seem to be simple', and while these series of short paragraphs summarizing the teaching of the holy fathers contain some things that the veriest beginner knows and understands, there is much that is beyond him: but the spirit informing them, the straightforward simplicity of expression, the imperturbable concern for 'the one thing necessary' give them an immediate and striking power. It is 'pure spiritual milk' indeed, whose very read-

[1] *Early Fathers from the Philokalia*, translated from the Russian text by E. Kadloubovsky and G. E. H. Palmer (London, 1954), pp. 283-346; *The Ascetic Life. The Four Centuries on Charity*, translated from the Greek text by P. Sherwood (London and Westminster, Md., 1956).

ing encourages that 'passionlessness' (*apatheia*)[1] to which Maximus, as a good Easterner, returns again and again. We Westerners, with our dim or lively recollection of Quietism, our instinct to be up and doing, are apt to fight shy of 'passionlessness', to be suspicious of it. But St Maximus himself warns the reader not to read in order to 'contradict and confute . . . but to weigh and consider' (as Francis Bacon said of studies in general), otherwise 'nothing useful will ever be revealed in anything'; and the Centuries, read 'with fear of God and love', allay our fears and calm our restlessness.

Like many other great spiritual writers, Maximus was addressing himself to dedicated religious, monks and nuns; but the principles of Christian life are the same for everybody, and whether consciously or not, these writers were, *mutatis mutandis*, also addressing anybody who would give heed to them. Monks and nuns take on many voluntary deprivations for the sake of the Kingdom; but, says Maximus, 'The Scriptures do not deprive us of anything given by God for our use, but curb immoderation and correct lack of judgement. In other words they do not forbid eating, bearing children or having money and spending it rightly, but they do forbid gluttony, adultery and so on. They do not even forbid us to think of these things—for they are made to be thought about—but they forbid thinking passionately of them' (4th Century, 66). 'We are virtuous or sinful according to whether we use things sensibly or stupidly' (I. 92). Again and again in these ancient religious writers the reader is struck by their 'contemporariness' and by the relevance of their teaching to the needs of the Christian today: and perhaps not least in

[1] *Apatheia* does not mean passivity or insensibility, still less apathy, but it is difficult to define. Though expressed by negatives—passionlessness, unmovedness, unimpassionedness—it has a positive quality.

this, that they expound adult teaching in an adult way ('adult' does not mean 'highbrow'), and they respect the mind and responsibility of their hearers. They offer nothing mechanical, no 'short cut', no 'easy way': Christian life is made to appear what it is—a most difficult undertaking for anybody, be he monk or lay person. But, as one of them wrote, 'Actions that are pleasing to God are helped by the whole of creation'.

ST THEODORE THE STUDITE
Abbot

There is a large number of Theodores in the calendars and martyrologies, but it cannot be said that any of them are very well known. The most 'popular', though now hardly remembered in the West, is the martyr St Theodore the Recruit (Tiro), about whom little enough is known, and St Theodore of Tarsus and Canterbury is not forgotten in England: the greatest of them all, Theodore the Studite, is not even a name to most people—yet he was a notable ascetic teacher and confessor of the faith, and as a monastic legislator has an importance that puts him in the front rank of Eastern influences.

He was born at Constantinople in 759, into a wealthy family of good position (his father was a treasury official), and was much influenced by his mother, who was a woman of intelligence and wisdom. The details of his early education are not known, but it was sound and included a good deal of theological reading. When he was twenty-two he became a monk at Sakkoudion in Bithynia, where his uncle, St Plato, was abbot; he was ordained priest some years later, and in 794 became abbot in place of his uncle, who had resigned. Almost at once there took place his first collision with the civil power.

The young emperor Constantine VI had embroiled himself with the Church by repudiating his wife and enter-

ing into a union with one Theodota, and in the resulting
dispute he was anxious to have the support of the abbot of
Sakkoudion, probably because Theodota was a near
relative of Plato and Theodore. The Sakkoudion monks
were only anxious to be left alone and not involved in a
matter that had all sorts of political ramifications, but,
when pressed by the emperor, St Theodore had to reply
that he and his monks could not support their sovereign in
this matter. Hints of reward and veiled threats did not
avail, and when Constantine went to take the waters at
Brusa, near Sakkoudion, and looked for Theodore to pay
him a ceremonial visit there, nobody from the monastery
turned up. The emperor, more to vindicate his outraged
dignity than with any hope of coercing Theodore, issued
an order for the deportation of the abbot and his principal
supporters. The aged Plato was shut up in the monastery
of St Michael at Constantinople and Theodore taken to
Salonika. From there he wrote an account of the journey,
hardships and good reception of himself and his companion
Joseph, a letter full of a rather nervous courage and of
admiration and affection for his old master. But the exile
lasted only a few months, being brought to an end by a
characteristic example of the brutal violence of the time
and place. In 797 the emperor's mother, Irene, dethroned
her son and had his eyes put out, and among the sub-
sequent actions of this 'God-beloved empress' was to recall
the Sakkoudion monks: the occasion of their restoration
must have deprived it of all element of rejoicing, or we
must hope it did. Theodore reassembled his scattered
flock, but in 799 decided to migrate to within the walls of
Constantinople, as the position of Sakkoudion was too
exposed to the raids of Arabs. The move was carried out
and he was given the buildings and governance of the
monastery of Studius.

St Theodore the Studite

This monastery[1] had its name from a certain Studius who had been consul at Rome in 454 and, coming to Constantinople, had founded the monastery in 463. It had already achieved fame as a centre of the so-called sleepless monks (they sang the Divine Office in relays all round the clock) and as a stronghold of orthodoxy against Monophysism, but the community had been scattered by the emperor Constantine Copronymus and there were only some dozen monks left in the place when St Theodore took it over: when he died twenty-seven years later they numbered a thousand in the monastery and its dependencies.

The specific constitutions (*typikon*) given by St Theodore to his monks have been the most important influence in Eastern monasticism after the general principles laid down by St Basil. St Athanasius (see page 101) introduced them in part on Mount Athos, and they were adopted and adapted far and wide.[2] Among the matters upon which St Theodore was insistent were the primacy of worship, community life (i.e., cenobitical as opposed to eremitical), manual work, learned studies and the fine arts. To provide a skeleton or framework for his community he established a hierarchy of officers, each of which was responsible for his work to the abbot; though there was apparently no formal school in connection with the monastery, teaching and intellectual occupations were eagerly promoted. 'Is it work time?' said Theodore. 'Then, to your labour. Is it

[1] It is often called the Stoudion, Studion or Studium, but there is no historical warrant for this name.

[2] There was a revival of Studite monasticism among the Catholic Ukrainians after 1901, when Metropolitan Andrew Szepticky founded a monastery in then Austrian Galicia. Despite setbacks it prospered greatly and expanded, but all its houses were suppressed by the Soviet government after 1945. A small group of refugee monks has made a fresh start in Canada.

leisure time? Then, to your studies'; and of manual arts that for which the monastery became most famed was calligraphy. In this Theodore was himself a master: one of his biographers refers to books beautifully written by the abbot's hand, and in a letter he expresses the pleasure and recreation that he found in copying manuscripts.

For the maintenance of the religious spirit of his monks St Theodore put much reliance on the catechetical discourses, 'conferences', which he gave; a number of them were later collected together as the Big and Little Catechisms. They are all short and very much to the point, and informed with a quiet but burning enthusiasm and conviction. Among the things with which no monk must have anything to do he emphasized slavery, an institution then still far from dead in Christendom. Not infrequently he is reminiscent of St Benedict: for example, in advising a hermit about physical asceticism, in which compared with most Eastern teachers he was notably moderate, he said, 'Don't cultivate a self-satisfied austerity. Eat bread, drink wine occasionally, wear shoes, especially in winter, and take meat when you need it.' Except for treatises on the veneration of images he wrote no theological works, but he left a number of sermons, letters (the chief source of his biography), poems and liturgical hymns. Of his epigrams— on saints, churches, the abbess Irene, a recluse, the place of his captivity, etc.—the byzantinist Karl Krumbacher says: 'It was specially due to him that the art of epigram, which in the dark days from the middle of the seventh to the end of the eighth century had fallen into desuetude, was recalled to life and by skilful application to things of present interest made worthy of continued existence.'

For eight years Theodore peacefully directed his growing monastery amid the turmoil of imperial politics, and then the affair of Constantine's adultery came up again, forerunner of yet more serious troubles. To fill the vacant patriarchal see of Constantinople the emperor Nicephorus I (who had deposed Irene in 802), chose his namesake, afterwards St Nicephorus, who was a layman at the time. For this reason St Theodore, St Plato and other monks opposed the appointment, and were imprisoned for twenty-four days in consequence. Then, at the request of the emperor, Nicephorus and a small synod of bishops reinstated the priest Joseph, who had been degraded for blessing the union between Constantine VI and Theodota. St Theodore and others refused to hold communion with Joseph or to accept the decision of a second synod that the marriage had been valid, and he, his brother Joseph, archbishop of Thessalonica, and Plato were relegated to Princes' Island (Prinkipo) and shut up in separate prisons. Theodore wrote to Rome explaining matters to the pope, and Leo III replied, commending his prudence and constancy; but the other side had spread rumours in Rome that Theodore was heretical and was annoyed at not having been made patriarch, and Leo made no formal judgement. The Studite monks were dispersed among other monasteries and grievously ill-treated, and the imprisonment of the leaders lasted nearly two years, until the death of the emperor Nicephorus in battle in 811.

A reconciliation was then brought about between Theodore and the patriarch Nicephorus, which was cemented by their unity in face of a fresh outbreak of Iconoclasm, the heresy that the veneration of images of our Lord and of his Mother and the other saints is unlawful.[1] In the year 726 a decree of the emperor Leo III, the Isaurian, had led to a wholesale destruction of images and persecution of their defenders, and the matter had been resolved in 787 by the seventh oecumenical council, at

[1] The images in question were not statues but the flat painted pictures (*eikons*) and mosaics usual in the East (and largely in the West at that date).

Nicaea, which decreed that the veneration of images is lawful, the respect paid to them being only relative and for the sake of what they represent. Then in 814 the cause of Iconoclasm was taken up again by the emperor Leo V the Armenian, a man of whom deservedly hard words have been used, but who seems to have had some better qualities than his predecessor and namesake, the Isaurian; nor can it be denied that there was enough superstitious abuse associated with the veneration of images to give a certain justification to its opponents: St Epiphanius was not the only one to condemn the misuse of images as idolatry. But it is one thing to attack an abuse, and quite another to try to remedy it by imposing false doctrine. In any case imperial Iconoclasm was in its origins not an end in itself, but a means to very important objects which had both political and religious significance. The civil and military authorities had needed the wholehearted support against the threatening Arabs of certain peoples and their bishops in Asia Minor, who attributed Christian military failures to Christian religious failures, especially superstition about images. Persecution of the defenders of their veneration became bitter, especially under Constantine V, which in turn had encouraged fanaticism in the persecuted, who found their most powerful support in the monasteries.

St Theodore openly denied any right of the emperor to interfere in religious matters, and on the Palm Sunday after the imprisonment of St Nicephorus by Leo's command, the abbot ordered all his monks to take images in their hands and to carry them in public procession, singing a hymn which begins, 'We reverence your holy image, O blessed one'. From this moment Theodore was recognized as the leader of the orthodox, and he continued to encourage all to honour holy images, for which the emperor banished him too. He was confined at Metopa in Asia Minor, and from there wrote to encourage the others

who were being persecuted. In one of his letters he condemns the calling of a synod by the intruded patriarch
Theodotus as being an action against the seventh oecumenical council, and also against that episcopal throne of
which it was promised that 'upon this rock I will build my
church'; in these and other writings on the subject
Theodore goes deeply into the implications of Iconoclasm:
he does not exhaust them, but he realizes the heresy's
affinities with Manichaeism (which taught the intrinsic
evil of matter) and thence with the monophysite error that
our Lord had not a human as well as a divine nature. In
the hope of checking the influence he was exercising
through these letters (he was probably enabled to send
them through the good offices of friends or through bribes
to jailers), Theodore was presently moved further away, to
Bonita, with the additional instruction that he should be
beaten on account of his activities. His jailer Nicetas
apparently realized that, since the letters were got away
through his own carelessness or venality, it was himself
who deserved the beating and had qualms of conscience
accordingly (or else he was susceptible to inducements);
for we are told that he contrived to give the impression of
thrashing his prisoner without actually doing so. This, or
something like it, happened a second time.

And so St Theodore still went on writing letters (many
of them are extant) to his monks and others, including the
patriarchs of the East and Pope Paschal I, to whom he
says: 'Listen, O apostolic bishop, shepherd appointed by
God over the flock of Jesus Christ. You have received the
keys of the kingdom of Heaven: you are the rock on which
the Church is built: you are Peter, since you fill his see.
Help us.' The pope in reply sent legates to Constantinople
(who, however, achieved nothing) and Theodore sent a
letter of thanks, in which he writes: 'You are from the
beginning the pure source of the orthodox faith; you are

the haven of the Universal Church, the shelter against the storms of heretics, the city of refuge chosen by God.'

For three more years St Theodore and his faithful attendant Nicholas were imprisoned at Bonita with extreme rigour, enduring great cold in winter and almost stifled in summer and tormented with hunger and thirst, for their guards for a time threw them only a little bread every other day. Theodore says that he expected they would very soon die of hunger, adding 'God is yet but too merciful to us', and they probably would have, had not a court official who passed that way been shocked by their condition and ordered them to be properly fed. The emperor, having intercepted another letter in which Theodore encouraged the faithful to defy the image-burners, ordered the prefect of the East to punish its writer. This officer was not won over as Nicetas had been, and had Nicholas, who had written out the letter, cruelly scourged and then a hundred stripes were given to Theodore, who was left lying on the ground exposed to the cold of February. He was for a long time unable to eat or sleep, and was only saved by the care of Nicholas who, in spite of his own sufferings, fed him drop by drop with soup and did his best to dress his wounds. Before he was properly recovered an officer arrived to take him and Nicholas to Smyrna, in 819, five years after their confinement had begun at Metopa. They had to walk during the daytime and at night were put in irons. At Smyrna the archbishop, a bitter iconoclast, kept Theodore confined closely for over eighteen months, under conditions that were even more severe than before.

In 820 Leo V was murdered, and in a church at that, an event at which Theodore's satisfaction, as expressed in his letters, is more understandable than edifying. The new emperor was Michael II the Stammerer, who favoured the iconoclasts but showed, perhaps under the pressure of the

St Hilarion overcoming the Serpent

detail from the fresco by Pietro Lorenzetti, Pisa

Titian: Chiesa de S. Giovanni Elemosinario, Venice

St John the Almsgiver, as imagined in the west

political situation, a more tolerant spirit. At the beginning
of his reign the exiles were recalled and St Theodore was
released after seven years of imprisonment. He wrote a
letter of thanks to Michael, exhorting him to be reconciled
with Rome, the head of the churches, and through Rome
with the other three patriarchs (Alexandria, Antioch and
Jerusalem), and freely to permit the veneration of images.
But the emperor refused to allow any *eikons* in the imperial
city or to restore the patriarch Nicephorus or any other
orthodox prelates to their offices, for he saw behind the
attitude and actions of St Theodore and his followers a
determined effort to create a systematic restraint on the
arbitrary exercise of the imperial authority, especially in
ecclesiastical affairs. Theodore, after making fruitless re-
monstrances, left Constantinople and visited the monasteries of Bithynia to encourage and strengthen his
followers, but he was disappointed at Michael's attitude:
'The winter is over,' he wrote, 'but why is spring not yet
come? The sky is clearer and there is hope of a good
passage, but ... The fire is out—why is there still smoke?'
But his own personal influence was so great that monks in
general and Studites in particular were regarded as
synonymous with orthodoxy, and he had many influential
adherents in and around Constantinople, including the ex-
empress Mary. For a time he seems even to have been
allowed to return to the monastery of Studius, apparently
for fear that otherwise his monks might give their support
to a revolt that was in progress; but after the danger was
past, and the emperor would still restore neither images to
the churches nor St Nicephorus to his see, St Theodore
again retired from the city.

He was now sixty-seven years old, and worn out with
work and years of harsh imprisonment. Driven by Arab
forays from one monastery, he went for rest to that of St
Trypho on the promontory of Akrita. He was taken ill in

the beginning of November 826, yet walked to church on the fourth day, which was Sunday, and celebrated the Holy Mysteries. His sickness increasing, he dictated what is called his testament, which includes a profession of faith and instructions for his monks, and spoke to a great number of persons who came to visit him. He celebrated the Liturgy for the last time on the Tuesday, and died amid his brethren on the following Sunday, November 11. His body was translated to his monastery eighteen years after his death.

St Theodore the Studite is greatly venerated in the East, and is named in the Roman Martyrology as 'famous throughout the Church', as indeed he well deserves to be, as a monastic leader, an upholder of the authority of the Holy See, and a spirited defender of and sufferer for the veneration of holy images. The Byzantines, Catholic and Orthodox, keep his feast on November 11.

St Theodore opposed the iconoclasts essentially on theological grounds. He did not regard sacred images as a necessary artistic adornment of a church: he discouraged the pictorial representation of the virtues and vices, and any other 'unauthorized flights of the religious fancy'. Nor did he deem their veneration a *necessary* devotional exercise; he seems to have used it but little himself, regarding it simply as an aid to devotion for the 'weaker brethren'. In his own instructions on prayer he sees the heart and mind in direct communion with God without reference to any exterior helps or intermediaries. But he saw clearly that to deny the lawfulness of the display and veneration of holy images was to deny the validity of certain theological principles which are essential to the Christian faith. As has already been said, many of his writings have come down to us, including over 500 letters, treatises on monastic life and the veneration of images, sermons and a number of hymns. Like the life of the saint, they are marked with that rigorism and uncompromising detachment from the world, almost amounting to 'puritanism', which was characteristic of many of his followers, and in some of his successors was so exaggerated as gravely to disturb the Church's peace.

However, there was a less rigid side to his character, as may be seen in some of his letters to private individuals and about personal concerns. There have at all times been monks who look on the secular state of the ordinary Christian with something almost amounting to contempt, as a way of life permitted to man on account of his weakness, instead of as what it is, the normal way of life ordained by God for mankind. Not so St Theodore. He set a very high value on domestic life, and knew that holiness was not confined to the cloister. He wrote to a layman: 'These things that I have mentioned are the things that pertain to the true Christian, and do not imagine, Sir, that they are only the concern of monks: they are most strictly enjoined on monks but they are the concern equally of the laity at large—except, of course, celibacy and voluntary poverty, and there are times for abstinence and rules for self-denial regarding even these.' And to another: 'Every Christian ought to be as it were a reproduction of Christ, related to him as the branch is to the vine or a bodily member to the head.' To a man who had lost his third young child he wrote: 'It is sad for you, most sad. But it is far from being so for those who have been taken at so young an age that they were untouched by sin; theirs is a blessed and perfect life in the bosom of Abraham, where they glorify God with sweet song in company with the Holy Innocents and all the other Christ-bearing children.'

He advised an abbess not to worry about what was done in this or that other convent, since we should test ourselves by our own standards and not by those of other people. And a laywoman who had asked how often she ought to receive holy communion was told to use her own discretion. In another letter he protests against the injustice and uncharitableness of avoiding the company of a family on account of the sin—suicide—of one of its members, and, what is a little surprising in that time and place, he strongly objected against physical punishment, much more against execution, of heretics; he reminds his correspondent that Christ's sufferings are offered for the sake of sinners and declares that he, Theodore, would rather lose his own head than that a heretic should be beaten. It is inevitable that this should be compared with his attitude to the murder of the emperor Leo V—but even saints are not immune from inconsistency, and contradictory extremes were a characteristic of Byzantine life.

For a time the monastery of Studius maintained its prestige and influence, and under Abbot Nicholas (the same monk who had been with St Theodore during his imprisonment) opposed the doings of Photius; but during the tenth century it began to decay somewhat, and one of its monks was a violent partisan of Michael Cerularius. It was sacked by the Latins during the iniquities of the Fourth Crusade, was rebuilt, and began again to flourish during the fourteenth century, when its archimandrite had precedence over all others in the imperial city; it at last came to a miserable end when the Turks took Constantinople in 1453.

ST ATHANASIUS THE ATHONITE
Abbot

The most easterly of the three long narrow headlands
which the Khalkidike peninsula thrusts out into the
Aegean Sea is marked at its landward end by the remains
of the canal which Xerxes cut through it in the fifth century
before Christ; at its other end, some thirty-five miles away,
a mountain towers up 6,000 feet, and it is by the name of
this peak, Mount Athos, that the promontory is commonly
known; but throughout the Near East it is called the Holy
Mountain, Hagion Oros, a little state (now part of the
kingdom of Greece) populated by monks. For a thousand
years it has been the chief centre of Byzantine monasticism.
The beginnings of monasticism at Athos are shrouded in
legend; it is said to have been a haunt of Christian hermits
from the fifth century, though there is no definite mention
of them in history till considerably later than that. The
monks were involved in the general separation of the
Eastern church from the West in the later middle ages,
and they submitted to the Turks after the fall of Constantinople in 1453, but all the time the purely monastic
character and semi-sovereignty of Athos were maintained.
It became a usual place of retreat for emperors, bishops,
and others in days of misfortune, at times a sort of con-
centration-camp for them.

The founder of Mount Athos as a federation of

organized monasteries was born at Trebizond, on the south-eastern coast of the Black Sea, about 925. He was the son of a good family from Antioch, and was baptized Abraham. He was left an orphan at an early age and in his youth was adopted by an imperial tax-collector, who took him to Constantinople: here charge was taken of him by a certain general, who was a relative by marriage. Abraham was a promising scholar and in time was raised to professorial rank, but he gave up his chair (it is said because he found his lectures to be attracting students away from his former master) and accompanied his guardian on an expedition to the Aegean, where he saw from afar and for the first time the shining peak of Athos. On his return to Constantinople, uncertain what he was going to do in the world, but drawn toward a life of solitude, there occurred the decisive moment of his life: he met St Michael Maleinos, abbot of Kymina, and with him his nephew Nicephorus Phocas, later on to be emperor.

The conversation of the monk confirmed Abraham's inclination to withdraw from the world, he went back with him to Kymina (on the borders of Bithynia and Paphlagonia), and was there clothed with the angelic habit, as monastic dress is called in the East, and received the name Athanasius. After four years of community life he was allowed to become a hermit in the neighbourhood of the monastery, and when Nicephorus Phocas and his brother Leo paid their uncle a visit the abbot appointed Athanasius to be their spiritual father, 'spiritual director' as we should say. The same was done with respect to several other distinguished people, and Athanasius soon realized with alarm that there was every prospect of his being appointed abbot when Michael Maleinos should die; he was already over sixty and Athanasius thought there was no time to be lost, so one night in the year 958 he slipped away and made his way to Mount Athos.

Changing his name to put off any hue and cry that might be raised, he as it were apprenticed himself to an old hermit, just as if he were not already himself a solitary of some experience. He even pretended he could not read and write, and shammed stupid when his master tried to teach him. However, his identity was soon discovered, and fruitless efforts were made to draw him out of his solitude. Eventually, when Nicephorus Phocas was preparing an expedition against the Saracens, the general persuaded him to come to Crete and support it with his advice and prayers. This was the last sort of thing Athanasius wanted to do, but he went, and the military expedition was successful. He then got ready to return to Mount Athos. Before he did so Nicephorus told him that he wanted a hermitage built on the Holy Mountain where he himself would become a monk, and also a monastery near-by. This suggestion was not acceptable to Athanasius: he had fled from Kymina to escape the distractions of office, and here he was threatened with a yet bigger responsibility. Moreover, he knew something of these men of the world with an itch to be monks. 'No,' he said. 'Fear God, and take care amid the snares of the world. As for your future, leave it in God's hands.'

But after he got back to Athos Athanasius received a large sum of money from Nicephorus, and, as he could not use it except as the giver had asked, he built a hermitage and chapel (they still exist) and a monastery adjoining; he called it a *laura*, the name then reserved for monasteries wherein the monks lived in separate cells grouped more or less closely round their church. His biographer, who was a monk under Athanasius's successor, calls particular attention to the founder's ingenuity in bringing water by pipes from a source eight miles away. The monastery was finished in 963 and dedicated to God in honour of the Blessed Virgin Mary, but it is now called after its founder or, more often, simply *Lavra*, 'The Monastery'. It was the first regular monastery on the Holy Mountain.

Once Athanasius had made up his mind that he must put aside his wish to be a hermit and accept the burdens of being an abbot, he carried out his duties with extreme thoroughness. He drew up regulations (*typikon*) for all the aspects of monastic life, for the Divine Office, food and fasting, every-day behaviour, administration; and though he partly abandoned the strictly communal life of the Studites (provision was made for monks to attain to a properly solitary life), he took a great deal from the regulations of St Theodore. The life was extremely austere, the normal food, for example, being uncooked vegetables with oil, and not much of them, and discipline was to be severely maintained. One rule was that things found lying about—writing materials, needles, knives and towels are specified—should be hung up in the porch of the church so that there should be no excuse for a monk running round from cell to cell looking for something he had lost. Athanasius was particularly stern with the monk who should quarrel with, much less strike, another: 'One God, one faith, one baptism, one people, one church, and one holy habit: how then can anyone dare to rend the name of Christ and those who bear it—that is, to say one is of Paul and another of Kephas and another of Apollo? [cf. I Cor. 1: 12-13] Such a one has been tonsured with the scissors of Satan.'

No mention is made of studies in his regulations, though emphasis is laid on the importance of reading and understanding the Bible. And when he found that many of his subjects were illiterate, Athanasius had rooms set apart to which they could go after the evening office and hear the Scriptures read and expounded. His delicate touch in dealing with beginners is illustrated by the story of a novice who had committed some fault and was ashamed to admit

it. In an assembly of the monks, Athanasius fixed the
fault on an innocent old senior and asked him if he wasn't
ashamed of himself for falling into the mistakes of
beginners. The old monk said that he was, and the
youngster, touched by his elder's humility, got up and
publicly accused himself. Miracles were inevitably attributed to St Athanasius, and his biographer declares with
a sigh that 'the Father's spiritual combats, marvels, and
religious graces were so many that it is impossible to relate
them all'. Like biographers of later ages he took refuge in
favourably comparing his hero with some of the world's
greatest men: Athanasius had, for example, 'Joseph's
wisdom, Jacob's simplicity, Abraham's hospitality', and so
on, with our Lord, Moses, and Arsenius, Sabas, Pachomius, Antony—the great names of early monasticism.
Athanasius was not all that, but his work on Mount Athos
was of profound importance in the history of Eastern
monks.

In the summer of 963 Nicephorus Phocas was proclaimed emperor by his troops: nothing more had been
heard of his monastic ambitions, and in a month or two
he married the widow of his predecessor, a woman of not
entirely unblemished reputation. St Athanasius was not
pleased by these happenings: he had given up his solitude
under pressure from his spiritual son, and now it was made
as good as certain that Nicephorus would never occupy the
place prepared for him at Athos. It is not clear what happened next. One account says that Athanasius forsook his
foundation and spent some time among the monasteries of
Cyprus and Asia Minor. In any case he eventually came
to Constantinople and the presence of the emperor, whom
he rebuked for changing his mind about serving God as a
hermit, and added some good advice concerning the duties
of his new state. Nicephorus pleaded 'reasons of state' and
said he hoped to come and live on the Holy Mountain one

day. Then, expressing his sorrow for having caused Athanasius so much trouble, he sent him back to Athos with a sum of money to pay for the construction of a harbour, which was much needed there.

From the time that St Athanasius began the establishment of the monastery a lot is heard of the difficulties made for the founder and his enterprise by the agency of evil spirits. This is, in part, his biographer's picturesque way of referring to the local opponents of Athanasius. He had introduced a communal organization among the inhabitants of the Holy Mountain and, though his monks maintained much of the older solitary tradition, he was vehemently opposed by the anchorites and hermits who with their predecessors had been there long before his arrival. They looked on him as an interloper, who had come uninvited into their 'desert' and was now claiming authority and organizing and building and upsetting their life and ideas in all directions. How little some of them had profited by leading a life of exterior perfection is shown by the fact that they resorted to criminal violence, and on two occasions even attempted to murder Athanasius. But they got no satisfaction when they appealed to the emperor John Tzimiskes,[1] complaining that Athanasius 'upsets our traditional laws and alters the old customs of the mountain'. The emperor made inquiry and then confirmed the gifts and rights granted by his predecessor, forbade opposition to Athanasius, and recognized his authority over the whole of the mountain and its inhabitants.

Thus by the time of his sudden death St Athanasius had become general superior over numerous communities and quasi-communities of monks and hermits. Men came to the Holy Mountain from all over the Near East, and even

---

[1] Nicephorus Phocas had been assassinated in 969, victim of a plot between his wife Theophano and his nephew John Tzimiskes.

from Italy, and, in addition to Lavra itself, the monasteries of Iviron, Vatopedi and Esphigmenou, founded during his lifetime, still exist as living communities.

On July 5, about the year 1003, St Athanasius gave a conference to his monks; his closing words stand as it were as his last will and testament to them: 'My brothers and children,' he said, 'we must keep watch over our tongues: it is better to fall from a high place than to sin by spoken words. Expect to be tempted, for through temptation and wrongs suffered we enter the kingdom of Heaven. Do not be dismayed when troubles threaten but remember that difficulties are useful to us, for man sees things in one way, but they are used by God in another.' He then, to the surprise of all, put on the cloak and hood which had been given him by St Michael Maleinos, which he wore only on great feast days, and went out with half a dozen of them to inspect the rebuilding going on in the church. Together they went up on to a scaffolding in the sanctuary, and as they reached the top the roof of the cupola fell in without a second's warning. Five of them were killed instantaneously, the architect Daniel was rescued alive but mortally hurt, and they worked feverishly to get at Athanasius, whose voice could be heard beneath the debris. At the end of three hours they released him, but he was dead. No external injury was visible, except that one foot had been crushed beneath a beam.[1]

After relating some of the miracles that took place at the saint's tomb his biographer ends his narrative with words that can be adapted to the needs of any Christian: 'There, blessed Father, are the things that made up your life and your death, and those that you did after your death, and how you did them. We members of your flock are still

[1] That Athanasius had foreseen that his death was at hand is shown not only by his putting on festal clothes; it was clearly implied in a statement made to one of his monks.

earth-bound, and open to the attacks of evil spirits and of wicked men: we need your help and intercession before the throne of God. You loved us with all your heart, for our sakes you worked and were weary, you lived for us until the end, and then you died for us: on our knees we beg you not to cease interceding for your children with God, who is the friend of man. You know the difficulties and fears that beset us, the malice of demons, the insurgence of the flesh, the heedlessness of human will and its inclination towards evil: we beseech you, then, to be our light, our guide and our saving master in this grievous and deceitful life. Look down from your place before the Trinity and guide us so that we may live in peace and tranquillity here below, and find at the last a loving and merciful Judge, to whom be glory and honour with his uncaused Father and their common Spirit, now, always and for ever and ever.'

St Athanasius the Athonite, who is sometimes called 'the Lauriote' or 'of Trebizond', is named daily in the preparation of the Byzantine Liturgy; his feast day is July 5. The thousandth anniversary of the foundation of the Lavra is being celebrated in 1963. There are still on Mount Athos twenty 'ruling monasteries', twelve lesser houses, and numerous hermitages and groups of various kinds. But where monks and hermits were once numbered in their thousands, there are now only some 1600, the great majority of them Greek by nationality (there is also a number of lay servants and workmen). Nevertheless the Holy Mountain remains one of the most famous institutions of the Christian world and the monastic centre of the Orthodox Eastern Church; and there are not wanting signs, small but encouraging, that decline will be arrested and that it will continue to be a spiritual beacon for centuries to come.

ST JOHN THE IBERIAN AND ST EUTHYMIOS

Abbots

Among the monasteries founded on Mount Athos during the lifetime of St Athanasius was Iviron, so called because it was established by and for people from Iberia (Georgia). Its founders were St John, called 'the Iberian' or 'the Hagiorite' (i.e., the Holy-Mountain Man), and his son St Euthymios, called 'the Enlightener', who arrived on Athos somewhere about the year 970. There is still extant an account of these two saints written by the hieromonk (i.e., a monk who is also a priest) George, who was almost their contemporary at Iviron and became its abbot.

John belonged to a noble family and was distinguished alike for his personal attractiveness, military valour, intellectual ability and uprightness of life. In early middle age and at the height of his career he parted from his wife and family, gave up his fortune and his post in the service of David, ruler of the Iberians, and retired to a monastery among the many on Mount Olympus—not the one in Greece but in Bithynia, Asia Minor. While there he learned that his son Euthymios had been sent with other young noblemen as hostages to the emperor at Constantinople, and John forthwith went there in order to retrieve him. The emperor listened to the plea that Euthymios was an only son and he was allowed to depart, choosing to go back to Olympus with his father.

According to the biographer George, it was the attentions of many followers consequent on his growing reputation for holiness that drove John from Mount Olympus to the more remote shelter of Athos. The migration of monks has so often been attributed to this cause that one seems to see the nearer East and Europe covered for centuries with holy men fleeing from their disciples,[1] and at least some of these migrations can reasonably be attributed to a natural human desire for change. Whatever may have been the explanation in this case, to Athos John and Euthymios went, where they joined the community of St Athanasius, John for two years and more being in charge of the kitchen. Then there came in flight from the world to the Holy Mountain another well-known Iberian, the general John Thornikios, brother-in-law of St John, and for greater seclusion the three compatriots were allowed to build themselves cells and a chapel at a little distance from the main monastery.

Thus they lived in great content till about the year 979, when Bardas Skleros invaded Asia Minor and was seriously threatening the empire; the young emperor, Basil II the Bulgar-slayer, appealed to the veteran soldier Thornikios to come and help him.[2] Thornikios was disinclined to go, but the other John and St Athanasius persuaded him, not by an appeal to patriotism or anything like that but by the simple argument that 'If you do not obey the emperor you will provoke his anger against our monastery'. Unwillingly, and on the understanding that St Athanasius and St John should take the responsibility for his action, Thornikios went; he struck a political and

---

[1] Forgetful that the Lord sends disciples to great men in order (among other things) to keep the great men humble.
[2] Another soldier monk, Bardas Phocas, was brought out of his (forced) retirement on Khios: as he had been fighting in Iberia, it was probably he who thought of Thornikios.

business bargain between the empress regent, Prince David of Iberia and himself, and was given command of twelve thousand cavalry; with these he helped Bardas Phocas to defeat Skleros at the battle of Pankalia, and returned to Athos laden with booty—'that which belongs to a victorious general, gold, silver, rich clothes and all that kind of thing', says George. And that is how funds were forthcoming to build the monastery of the Blessed Virgin and St John the Baptist, called Iviron.

It was decided to establish this monastery because of the increasing number of Iberians who were coming to Mount Athos,[1] but from the first they had to admit Greek monks because, as George remarks, 'we know nothing about seafaring and many necessities had to be got by water', and there were not enough artisans, masons, carpenters and the rest, among the Iberians to do all the work required. The monastery was duly built and there were enough funds left over to give some valuable presents to the *laura* of St Athanasius, including a number of books, holy images, church vessels, four mules, three horses and a boat.

Thornikios was treated with respect by his companions (not, we hope, simply because he was the chief benefactor), but he seems to have been a characteristically garrulous old soldier: he spent so much time talking with visitors about the wars and his old friends (there is a suggestion that his conversation was not always free from profanity) that at last notice had to be taken of it. St John gently remonstrated and put him under obedience to talk freely only with a respectable old monk, named Gabriel. Thornikios expressed his penitence and is said never to have offended in this way again. But the death of the ex-general came as a relief in more ways than one. John had never been really

---

[1] The vigour of the monastic life of the early Georgian church extended to Syria, Palestine, Sinai, Asia Minor, Greece and its islands.

enthusiastic to start the new *laura*, and now his friend was no longer there to share them, its bustle and worry were more than he could bear: he resolved to take flight, with his son and a few specially dear disciples, to Spain. They got as far as Abydos, when their movements were reported to the emperors Basil II and Constantine VIII, and they were ordered to Constantinople.

'Holy father,' said Basil, when they came into their presence, 'we have shown our regard for your goodness by great marks of esteem and affection. Why then do you run away and try to emigrate to a strange land?'

To which John replied: 'Religious and most mighty emperors, I am a poor layman, and I find myself badly off in this world, overcome by all sorts of wickedness. That is why I want to go to some far-off country, where I can concern myself with my soul's salvation. There I can live in poverty and get rid of the crowd of cares and visitors that came to me with the coming of my brother-in-law.' However, with great trouble he was persuaded to return to Athos and the government of Iviron, and back he went with his companions.

During the last years of his life St John was kept to his bed by gout and general debility; he bore his sufferings with patience, thanking God for sending him so painful an affliction. When his strength entirely failed he handed the government of the monastery over to his son, but till the end nothing was done without his authorization. On his deathbed, before the year 1002, he exhorted his brethren: 'Let nothing distract you from our holy work and from the love of God, that is, from humble obedience and a close harmony of souls; so will you be saved in this mortal life and gain for the future eternal life by the love which our Lord Christ bears towards human kind. May the merciful and all-pitiful God have mercy on you and lead you in the way of his divine teaching and holy will, by the intercession

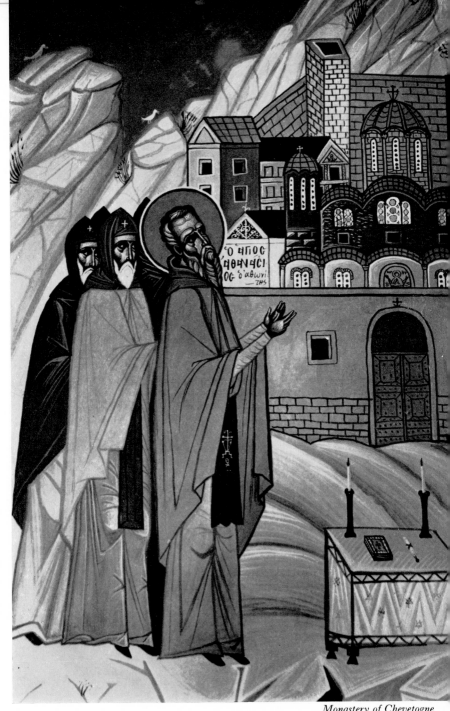

The inscription in the icon reads:

Ο ΑΓΙΟΣ
ΑΘΑΝΑCΙ
OC ὁ ἀθωνί
της

St Athanasius consecrating the first *laura* on Mount Athos

Lavra Monastery (above) and Iviron Monastery on Mount Athos

of the all-holy Mother of God and of all the saints. Amen. Never fail to receive guests well, and share with the poor, according as you are able, those things which God in his goodness has given you. Pray for me, my children and brethren, and do not forget me. . .' He asked the blessing of his son Euthymios, and peacefully gave his soul to God. Father George says of him: 'Truly was our blessed father John a man dear to God and worthy of all veneration. Like Abraham, he went forth from his own country to lead a life of exile and poverty. He gave himself into the hands of the spiritual fathers, and God made him the equal of those whom he took for his pattern.'

An interesting event happened on Athos while St John was alive, one in which he was concerned by giving hospitality to its initiators and encouragement and help to their work: this was the establishment of a Latin monastery under the Rule of St Benedict. It was founded by citizens of Amalfi in Italy and came to an end only in 1169. Small ruins of the abbey still remain, and its archives are in existence but up to the present have not been studied in detail. Father George speaks of the founder, Leo the Roman, as a brother of the duke of Benevento and refers to the good observance kept by the Benedictines at the time he was writing.

St Euthymios, who succeeded his father as abbot, was like him a physically handsome man, and he was strong as well: it was noted of him that he never used any support in church, but stood throughout the long offices with his hands crossed on his breast and his head slightly bent. He was modest and straightforward, and never made a statement on his own authority if he could find a biblical or other text to support it. This he was peculiarly well qualified to do, for he had spent years translating sacred books from Greek into Iberian; he knew both languages equally well. George's biography names over sixty works for which the Iberian church was indebted to the labours of Euthymios: among them are biblical commentaries, some of the writings of St Basil, St Gregory of Nyssa, St Ephrem, St John Damascene, St John Climacus and St Maximus the Confessor, the *Institutes* of St John Cassian and the *Dialogues* of Pope St Gregory, numerous lives of saints and martyrs and liturgical books. It seems that he also translated from Iberian into Greek the *History of Saints Barlaam and Joasaph*, a work now known to be nothing but a christianized version of the story of Siddartha Buddha; this text was formerly attributed to St John Damascene.[1]

Under the rule of this learned man the community of Iviron quickly increased in numbers, and others came to be hermits near the monastery. Some of these hermits suffered from an unattractive sort of spiritual perversion: when visitors made them presents they were anxious to give them away to those more needy, but would not do so with their own hands: 'We hermits,' they explained, 'are rather like immaterial beings, and God does not require such actions from so spiritualized persons.' But more troublesome to St Euthymios were the rich young aspirants who wanted to make fine gifts to the monastery and then lead a life of idleness there. The abbot refused both their gifts and their company.

A good deal of the hieromonk George's account of St Euthymios consists of details of the abbot's disciplinary methods and examples of his virtues, on a plan only too familiar to readers of hagiography—'The miracles of Euthymios . . . Humility of our saint . . . His spirit of poverty . . . Other edifying characteristics'; but they are less 'common form' than is usual with such eulogies and

---

[1] Unfortunately, Cardinal Baronius added the names of 'the holy Barlaam and Josaphat' to the Roman Martyrology (November 27), from which they have not yet been removed.

give details of daily life that are of value to students of monastic observance. It emerges that Euthymios was a firm but not severe superior, who kept an eye on the smallest details and relied as much upon silent example as spoken precepts: we are told, for instance, that he was never late for office in spite of the fact that his cell was some way from the church, apparently up several flights of stairs. He was what is nowadays called a teetotaller, a notable austerity in a land where wine was the ordinary drink of everybody and it was a matter of course for each monk to have it with his dinner; yet Euthymios was very particular about this wine. He would sip it every day before the meal, and if it were sharp or too diluted would remonstrate with the cellarer. 'Remember, brother,' he would say, 'that this is your brethren's only full meal. When the wine is strong, by all means water it down, but reasonably; when it is middling, add a little water; when it is poor, less or none.' To the procurator he gave instructions that beardless boys were not to be employed as workmen around the monastery, lest they have a demoralizing effect on the monks: 'I know that grown men must be given higher wages, but it is better to spend more money than to expose our brethren to possible harm.'

St Euthymios governed Iviron for fourteen years, during which time he refused promotion to the archiepiscopal see of Salamis in Cyprus. He eventually resigned his charge because, as is said, it was represented to him that the Iberians were badly in need of more of the translations which only he could do so well. But it was not easy to find an abbot who could govern so well either. A relative of Euthymios, George (not the biographer), was appointed, and the monastery was soon in a state of discord, largely due to George's partiality for the Greek brethren as against the Iberians. The scandal became public, and the emperor Constantine VIII sent for Euthy-

mios to come and give an explanation. Before leaving the
Holy Mountain he went to see a close friend, Father Theo-
phanes, who greeted him with tears. 'Alas!' he exclaimed,
' I shall never again see you in this mortal body.' And so it
was.

St Euthymios had to stay some time in Constantinople,
and on a day in May in the year 1028 he mounted his mule
to go and see about a painting of St John the Evangelist
which he had ordered. On the way he was stopped by a
beggar whose flapping rags and piercing cries startled the
mule: it plunged violently and Euthymios was thrown
heavily to the ground. He was carried into a neighbouring
monastery and was found to be seriously hurt, and there
within a few days he breathed his last. His body was taken
back to Mount Athos and buried at Iviron; his feast is
observed every year on May 13, that of his father St John
being on July 12.

Speaking of the monastery of Iviron the hieromonk
George says: 'This famous *laura*, magnificently built and
beautified with all kinds of decoration, was raised by these
blessed men with great labour and endless perseverance
to be a place of refuge for many souls. They built heavenly
churches, which they provided with sacred books and
venerable images. They endowed it with lands, with farms,
with dependencies and cells, and thus provided for the
fitting celebration of the Holy Mysteries. They obtained
protection and charters for it from the religious emperors.
And they gathered therein monks of angelic life who by
their translation of sacred texts became an ornament of our
country and the flower of our language.' As has been said,
this monastery of Iviron still exists, but it has long ago
passed from the hands of the Georgians into those of the
Greeks. Among its treasures is the wonder-working *eikon*
of the Mother of God, called *Portaitissa*, found washed up
on the beach, so the story goes, having been thrown into

the sea by iconoclasts at Constantinople. The famous Moscow *eikon* of our Lady of Iviron is a copy of it, made in 1648.

George finishes his long account of the two saints with an appeal for their prayers: 'Blessed father Euthymios, be merciful to us your servants, unhappy exiles and pilgrims here below. Intercede for us, that our numberless sins may be forgiven at Judgement-day, and that in this life we may be delivered from Satan's wiles and from the malice of men.

'And may I, Father George, be held in loving remembrance by his fellows.'

ST NEILOS OF ROSSANO
Abbot

Seven hundred years before the religion of Christ was given to mankind the people of Hellas began to plant colonies along the coasts of Sicily and southern Italy; these settlements became prosperous and powerful, and Calabria and Apulia, with parts of Sicily, were so hellenized that they are known in history as *Magna Graecia*, Greater Greece. This part of Italy was conquered by the Romans during the third century B.C., and after the division of the empire Justinian joined it to his eastern territories. Its inhabitants had received the Gospel at an early date, and from the eighth century these Greeks were accounted part of the Eastern church, under the patriarchal jurisdiction of Constantinople. This state of affairs came to an end after the Normans conquered southern Italy and Sicily in the early years of the eleventh century. From then on the local Greeks were little by little absorbed by their neighbours; and the Byzantine setting of their ancestral Christianity was very gradually exchanged for that of the West, till today the Italo-Greeks of Byzantine rite are reduced to a few tens of thousands of rather poverty-stricken peasants. Indeed, they would doubtless have disappeared altogether but for immigrations from Albania during the fifteenth and sixteenth centuries.

A century before the Norman invasion began, a child

was born into a good Greek family of Calabria[1] the principal achievement of whose life was destined to outlast the political, social and ecclesiastical vicissitudes of his people and to perpetuate the memory of Magna Graecia outside its own frontiers. His birthplace was Rossano, the year was about 910, and the boy was christened Nicholas. His early manhood, so far as it is known, was unpromising. He entered into a union with a woman who bore him a daughter, and it has been seriously questioned whether they were ever married; the weightier opinion appears to be that they were not. But when he was about thirty mother and child died, and Nicholas was stricken by a serious illness; when he recovered he had decided to serve God as a monk.

This was easier said than done, for he was a valued treasury official. But Byzantine monasteries were numerous in the south of Italy at that time and he was eventually given the habit at one of them, when he took the name of Neilos. The times were troubled, and over a period of forty years he lived in several monasteries and underwent trying experiences during Saracen raids. For a time he was a hermit, with two companions, and returned to his monastery only to have it pillaged by freebooting soldiers: they stole even his hairshirt, which seems a strange article to have attracted their attention. At length he became abbot of St Adrian's, near San Demetrio Corone (which is still a Byzantine centre).

Neilos had earned considerable reputation for wisdom and holiness of life, and he was frequently consulted by those seeking good advice. On one occasion he was visited by the archbishop of Reggio, Theophylact, and his chamberlain Leo, accompanied by several people who seemed more intent on sizing up the abbot and testing his knowledge than on profiting from his wisdom. Neilos

[1] Modern Calabria is the 'toe' of Italy; it was originally the 'heel'.

knew what they were after, but he received them courte-ously, took them into the church to pray, and then sat down to talk. He produced a book which he was reading and explained that its author set out to demonstrate that the number of souls who should be saved was necessarily small. This opinion the visitors found disagreeable, and they began to argue against it, whereupon Neilos quoted in its support passages from the Fathers and St Paul and the gospels themselves. 'These statements seem dreadful to you,' he said, 'but it is because they condemn the dis-order of your own lives. It seems to me clear that unless we be altogether holy we cannot escape everlasting punishment.'

Thereupon somebody inquired of Neilos whether King Solomon were damned or saved. The question was un-fortunately chosen, for the questioner was himself an adulterer, and Neilos knew it. 'What does it matter to us to know whether he be saved or not?' he replied. 'What does matter is to remember that Christ reprobates all those who commit adultery. For myself, I would rather know whether *you* are going to be saved.' Then, to cover his questioner's confusion, he added, 'As for Solomon, the Bible makes no mention of his repentance, as it does of that of Manasses.'

Another story of Neilos's way with men of the world and his influence over them concerns a nobleman named Euphraxus, who was sent into Calabria as governor. On his arrival most of the leading prelates, servile and time-serving men, sent him expensive presents, and among those who did not was the abbot of St Adrian's. Euphraxus noticed the omission and lost no opportunity of making himself a nuisance to St Neilos and his community. But when he had been very ill and terrifyingly near death he thought better of it: he went to Neilos and not only apologized for his behaviour but also asked to be admitted among his monks. He was refused, for, said the abbot, 'Your baptismal promises are quite sufficient without taking any monastic vows. Repentance does not call for them, but simply for a sincere determination to alter your way of living.' It is recorded that Euphraxus was not satisfied with this, but returned again and again to the monastery till at last, having freed all his serfs and given away most of his goods to the poor, he was clothed with the monastic habit three days before he died.

At about the age of seventy, when he might reasonably be looking forward to a quiet ending of his days in the monastery that he had governed so well, those events befell for which more than for any others St Neilos is remembered. The Saracen raids from Sicily into southern Italy were increasing in intensity, and at last the abbot and monks of St Adrian's decided that they must leave. They would have been welcomed in any part of the Greek world, for the name of Neilos had travelled far, but they decided instead to go further into Italy, which was closer at hand. So about the year 981 sixty of them, with Neilos at their head, set out towards the north and at Monte Cassino these representatives of Eastern monasticism threw themselves upon the hospitality of the headquarters of Western monasticism.

They were received with a generosity truly Benedictine, 'just as if', says the biographer of Neilos, 'St Antony had come from Alexandria or their own great St Benedict from the dead'. Accommodation was found for them and it was arranged that they should sing their Greek office in the abbey church when it was not in use by the Latin monks, in order that, as their host Abbot Aligern said, 'everything should be provided for their life, according to the word of God'. In his gratitude St Neilos wrote a hymn in honour of St Benedict, and learned Latin so that he could sometimes take part in the Western liturgy. (He was a writer of liturgical poetry, some of which has survived.) It was a time when the legitimacy of some Western disciplinary customs was being questioned by those who were inclined to separatism at Constantinople, and the monks of the two rites naturally discussed these matters. 'However we differ,' concluded Neilos, 'both do all things for the glory of God. Don't allow yourselves to be disturbed by these criticisms.'

The abbot of Monte Cassino bestowed on the fugitives the empty monastery of Vallelucio and there they lived for 15 years. Little is known of this period; but when in 990 the bishop of Prague, St Adalbert, later to be martyred, fled in desperation from his troublesome diocese, it was St Neilos who found him a home at the monastery of SS Boniface and Alexis on the Aventine at Rome, from where Pope John XV sent him back to his bishopric. The community's next move was to Serperi, near Gaëta, and from here in 998 Neilos made a visit to Rome. The emperor Otto III had just arrived in the city to deal with John Philagathos, bishop of Piacenza, whom the senator Crescentius had set up as antipope ('John XVI') against Gregory V. Neilos had in vain tried to dissuade Philagathos, who was a Calabrian Greek from Rossano like himself, from having any part in schism and treason, and the aged abbot now went to implore Otto and Gregory to have mercy on the fallen antipope; he had already been savagely mutilated by Otto's troops. Neilos was received with honour both by pope and emperor and listened to with respect, with the result that Philagathos was to be confined in a monastery instead of a prison. But such public indignities were heaped on the unhappy man that Neilos was moved to protest with considerable vigour. When a prelate was sent to explain matters, Neilos cut short his excuses by pretending to fall asleep.

In the following year Otto III visited the Greek monks

at Serperi. He was surprised to see the hard conditions in which these 'citizens of Heaven' lived, and offered to build a monastery for them within his own dominions and endow it. St Neilos thanked him and refused: 'If my brethren are truly monks,' he said, 'our divine Master will not leave them uncared for when I am gone.' Upon leaving, Otto pressed a purse of money upon the abbot, saying, 'Do not be afraid to ask anything you wish of me: I will gladly grant it. You went out in poverty in your younger days, but now that old age is upon you and death quite close you need not hesitate to accept this.' Neilos, deeply touched, laid his hand upon the emperor's breast and replied, 'I want only one thing of you, and that is that you should save your soul alive. You are emperor— but you must die and give an account to God just as other men.'

In the year 1004 or 1005, when he was well over ninety, St Neilos visited the monastery of St Agatha, south of Tusculum, and on his way home was taken ill at Grotta-ferrata, a small place on the lower slopes of the Alban Hills, said to be the spot where Cicero had a villa and wrote his *Quaestiones tusculanae*.[1] And here Neilos is said to have had a vision in which our Lady appeared and revealed to him that he had at last found the place where his monks were to have an abiding home. From Gregory, count of Tus-culum, he got a grant of land on Monte Cavo, and sent for his community to establish itself there. But before the work could be done he was dead. He was followed in quick succession as abbot by Paul and Cyril, and then came St Bartholomew of Rossano who, while St Neilos is rightly looked on as the founder of the abbey of Grottefarrata,

---

[1] According to local tradition, the place had its name from a shrine of our Lady in a cave, her picture being protected by an iron grating (in Latin, *Crypta Ferrata*).

was the man who completed the building and firmly established the community.

Bartholomew governed the monastery for many years before his death in 1055. He made it a centre for learned studies and the copying of manuscripts, himself being very skilled in the art of calligraphy. His vigorous government raised the Grottaferrata monastery to that position of importance from which it played a part in the history of the medieval papal states, a position which ultimately led to its decline as a religious house until its restoration during the seventeenth century. It was reformed again under Pope Leo XIII and still flourishes, its monks now being Italo-Albanian as much as Italo-Greek. It is still a place of learning, and among its contemporary activities which link it with the past is a workshop for the preservation and repair of manuscripts and books and the making of them legible: the monks have drawn upon the resources of chemistry and mechanics for their equipment, and from all over the world manuscripts and books that have suffered from sun, water, fire, worm, damp, misuse or sheer old age are sent for expert treatment. There is also a printing establishment, which has been responsible for the production of typical editions of Greek and Slavonic liturgical books of the Byzantine rite. Thus for nearly a thousand years there has been maintained a monastery of monks of the Byzantine rite and life within a few miles of the heart, not merely of the Latin, but of the Catholic world: a living and impressive testimony that 'the Church of Jesus Christ is neither Latin nor Greek nor Slavonic but Universal'. Its two founders are duly named in the Roman Martyrology, St Neilos, 'a man of great holiness', on September 26 and St Bartholomew on November 11. St Neilos is sometimes called 'the Younger' to distinguish him from an earlier saint of the same name.

ST BORIS AND ST GLEB
Sufferers

Seeing how few Russian lay people have been canonized, it is curious to find that the first saints formally canonized by the Church in Russia were two young laymen, whose title to sainthood, moreover, was questioned by some at the time, and has been the subject of no little discussion since. Their story is found in three separate accounts written within the century.

The first Christian prince of Kiev, St Vladimir, died in the year 1015. He left eleven sons, and the eldest, Svyatopolk, in order to safeguard his position, determined for a start to get rid of his two younger half-brothers, Boris and Gleb, Vladimir's sons by Ann of Constantinople.

Boris, who was less than twenty years old, was on his way back from a military expedition against the nomad Pechenegs when he learned of Svyatopolk's intention, and his array at once prepared to defend him. But Boris would not allow it. 'If he tries to kill me,' he said, 'I shall not resist. I shall then be a martyr, for the Apostle says that if any man claims to love God and yet hates his brother, he is a liar.' He would not raise his hand against an elder brother who now stood in the place of their father; like Christ, he would be an innocent victim rather than spill the blood of his brothers in the flesh and in God. Thereupon his warriors deserted him, and Boris, with a single companion, awaited events on the bank of the river Alta.

During the night he meditated on those martyrs who had been put to death by near relatives, on the emptiness of all earthly things 'except good deeds and true love and right religion', and he lamented that he must leave the 'marvellous light of day' and his 'good and beautiful body'. He fortified himself with the psalms of the night office, and one of his biographers professes to give the very words of the prayer he uttered before an *eikon* of the Saviour: 'Lord Jesus Christ, you who appear on earth in this image, who chose to be nailed to the cross and to suffer for our sins, give me strength to suffer too. Lord, do not impute this wickedness to my brother.'

Early in the morning a gang of ruffians arrived from Svyatopolk, and they set upon the young prince 'like wild beasts'. His attendant tried to defend him, and was at once killed. Weeping, Boris begged a few more minutes for his last prayer: 'Glory to you, my Lord, for enabling me to escape from the allurements of this deceitful life. . . For your sake I am led like a lamb to the slaughter. You see, my Lord, that I do not resist, I do not complain.' Then he turned to his murderers: 'Friends,' he said, 'now you can finish your work. Peace be to Svyatopolk my brother and to you.' They ran him through with their spears, then wrapped the body in a rug and took it away in a cart. But on the way Boris seemed to be still breathing, so he was stabbed through the heart.

Gleb was younger than Boris, and could hardly have been more than a boy. Svyatopolk, shamming friendliness, sent a message inviting him to Kiev, and he set off down the Dneiper. On the way a warning reached him from another half-brother, Iaroslav; but Gleb could not believe in Svyatopolk's treachery, and he continued his journey. Near Smolensk another boat was sighted, and he was 'heartily glad, expecting a welcome' from its occupants. But his boat was boarded by strange and threatening men,

armed with 'naked swords which glittered like the water'.
Gleb was terrified, and with tears streaming down his face
implored them: 'Do not harm me, dear friends, please do
not—I have done no harm to you! . . . Have mercy on me,
and you shall be my masters and I your slave!' When he
saw that appeals were useless he resigned himself to death:
'Better for me to be butchered as you were, Boris my
brother, than to live lonely and orphaned, without you.'
'I am to be slain,' he prayed, 'and I do not know why. But
you, Lord, my Lord, *you* know. You told your apostles that
hands would be laid on them for your name's sake, and
that men would be betrayed by their friends, and one
brother be given over to death by another.'

We are told that the fatal stroke was given by Gleb's
own cook, who crept up behind him and cut his throat,
'like a butcher killing a sheep, a meek lamb bringing a
clean sacrifice to the Lord'. His body was thrown contemptuously on to the river bank and left there.

What is to be made of this story? There seems to be no
serious ground for questioning that the murder of Boris
and Gleb by their half-brother actually took place, the first
move in a dynastic quarrel. But what of their sainthood?
They were victims of a purely secular ambition, they did
not die rather than renounce the Christian faith, which is
ordinarily the criterion of martyrdom.

From the nature of the case their thoughts and their
prayers to God, their final inward disposition of quiet re-
signation and determination not to resist evil by force,
could be known to none but themselves. The purport of
their meditations and the words of their prayers must have
been put into their minds and mouths by those who wrote
accounts of their end, the writer of the *Chronicle* and the
monk Nestor and another, said to be the monk Jacob. But
this does not necessarily mean that what these writers say
about the young princes' dispositions is worthless. On the

contrary, it represents what Russian Christians believed about them a generation or so after the events, and this belief could have a basis of truth in the knowable circumstances of those events.

The monk Nestor stresses the moral and political lesson to be drawn from the example of Boris and Gleb, when, for instance, he writes: 'You see how great was those saints' obedience to their elder brother. . . If they had resisted him, they would hardly have been granted such wonderful gifts. Nowadays there are many young princes who do not obey their elders, but oppose them: they too are killed, but they are not found worthy of such grace as those saints.' But the principal tenor of the victims' motives is represented as more purely religious, as a deliberate following of the Lord who rebuked Peter when he used the sword, who would not call on his Father for 'twelve legions of angels'. And it was this motive that prevailed and commended itself to the Russian people. They saw Boris and Gleb as *strastoterptsy*, sufferers (literally, 'passion-bearers'), innocent men who, unwilling to die, had yet repudiated violence and accepted death in the unresisting spirit of Christ and for his sake. 'You rejected the world's perishable glory. You underwent a wicked death without resisting the brother who slew you, for the sake of the spotless Lamb, the Saviour sacrificed for us.'

It was Vladimir's fourth son, Iaroslav, the same who had warned Gleb of his danger, who avenged his murdered brothers on Svyatopolk, and himself succeeded to his father's princedom of Kiev. After five years, in 1020, he buried the still incorrupt bodies of Boris and Gleb in the church of St Basil at Vyshgorod: their tomb became a place of pilgrimage and miracles were reported there, and their veneration has continued to this day. The Greek metropolitan was asked to declare their formal canonization, but he was more than dubious, for they did not fall

Theodosius
the Caves

*nastery of
vetogne*

ΘΕΟ
ΔΟ
СІЙ

ПЕЧЕ́РСКІЙ

Monastery of the Caves of Kiev

into any of the categories of saints with which he was familiar: they were not great ascetics, they were not bishops or teachers, they were not martyrs since they had not died for their faith. But popular feeling was so strong that the Greek ecclesiastical authorities submitted to what they did not understand, and Boris and Gleb were enrolled among the saints. This verdict was confirmed by Pope Benedict XIII seven centuries later, in 1724. They are sometimes referred to by their baptismal names, Romanus and David; their feast-day is July 24.

The veneration of slaughtered royal persons as martyrs is a not uncommon phenomenon. When it is a case of death in battle against the heathen it is easy to understand (St Oswald of Northumbria is an example); but it has happened with others besides St Boris and St Gleb whose death was compassed for dynastic or personal reasons. England again provides examples, in St Ethelbert of the East Angles and St Edward the Martyr. Nearly a century before Boris and Gleb, St Wenceslaus (Vaclav) of Bohemia had been killed by his brother for a motive of political ambition. This was not a case of unjust death accepted for evangelical reasons, but the precedent was known in Russia; indeed, one of the accounts of Boris and Gleb attributes to Boris advertence to the holy martyr Wenceslaus, as well as to St Nicetas and St Barbara.

ST THEODOSIUS OF
THE CAVES
Abbot

The earliest monasteries in Russia were more or less 'official' establishments, whose foundation was brought about by missionary Greek bishops with the help of the secular rulers; their influence was not destined to endure, but was soon displaced by that of a genuinely indigenous monasticism. The first specifically Russian monastery, whose contribution to Russian Christianity was very large indeed, was that of the Caves at Kiev (Kievo-Pecherskaya Lavra); its principal founder was St Theodosius, called 'of the Caves' (Pechersky), who is looked on as the father of Russian monasticism.

A year or two before the conversion of the grand-prince of Kiev, St Vladimir, in 989, there was born near Chernigov a child who grew up with a passionate desire for the solitary life. This Antony, learning by experience that one must be trained for this life as for any other, went to Mount Athos, where he became a hermit. After some years he returned to Russia, and took up his abode in a cave in a wooded cliff beside the river Dnieper at Kiev. Disciples gathered round him, who at first occupied other caves, and when their numbers increased built themselves cells and a church of wood: this was the beginning of the Monastery of the Caves.

St Antony soon gave up the direction of this community to one Barlaam and, after establishing another community at Chernigov, retired to his cave at Kiev; there he died at a great age in 1073. Meanwhile Barlaam had been quickly succeeded as abbot by St Theodosius, who held the office for many years and was the real organizer of the monastery of the Caves, giving their pattern to the first generations of Russian monks.

Theodosius had been born (the year is not known) at Vasilkov, some thirty miles from Kiev, of well-to-do parents. From the age of thirteen, when his father died, his ascetic habits earned him much obloquy from his mother, a woman 'of muscular body, with a voice like a man'. Her son was one of the first Russians to be fired with the desire to go on pilgrimage to the Holy Land, whither his fellow countrymen used to resort in such numbers before 1917; he never had his wish, but Palestine's influence on him was manifested in other ways later on. His mother was vexed because he 'demeaned himself' by wearing 'uncouth garb' and mortifying his body; and for over two years he worked as a baker, making altar-bread which he sold for the benefit of the poor, whose company he sought. So he was also a forerunner of those members of the Russian intelligentsia who 'went to the people' during the nineteenth century. When eventually he presented himself for admission among St Antony's monks at the Caves, his mother followed him and made a scene with the abbot; there were further painful interviews, but gradually she underwent a change of heart, and was even prevailed upon by her son's entreaties herself to become a nun.

After he was made abbot, St Theodosius completed the buildings and put the community under the discipline and rule given by St Theodore to the Studites. Emphasis was put, not on personal sanctification solely by means of prayer and penance, but on the necessity of corporal works of mercy and on the need of identifying oneself with all the suffering children of Christ. He followed both the liturgical prescriptions and the social activities of the Studites; a hospital for the sick and disabled and a hostel for travellers were established at the monastery, and every Saturday a cart-load of food was sent down to the city jails. Nor was Theodosius, as were so many early monks, afraid of contact with the ordinary world of men; his monks helped in evangelization, and he took part in the general life of the country, with the result that his influence was not confined to his community but was felt all over Varangian Russia: he was able to defend the rights of the poor and oppressed, and to protest to his face when Svyatoslav drove his own brother from the throne of Kiev. Moreover, to Theodosius may be traced the beginnings of the institution of *startsy*, elders, 'spiritual directors', so characteristic of Russian religious life; he encouraged lay people, without distinction of sex or age or rank, to come to him with their problems and difficulties, and we are told of a man and wife, of whom he was particularly fond, 'because they loved God and loved one another'.

Whereas St Antony Pechersky followed the Egyptian hermits, whose austerely isolated manner of life had a tendency to degenerate into fanaticism and even into a sort of competition in penances, St Theodosius Pechersky looked for his pattern rather to the monks of Palestine and such saints as Sabas and Euthymios the Great and his namesake Theodosius the Cenobiarch, who never forgot that physical austerity is only a means towards purity of heart and spirit. Virtue, goodness, closeness to God, is the aim of religion: the young, said Theodosius, must love their fellows and learn humbly and obediently from their elders; the old must love and help and teach the young, nor must any man make public his own penances. He emphasized, too, the importance of community life and the holding of all things in common, so much so that one of his monks declared that a 'Lord, have mercy on us' prayed from the heart collectively by the community is of greater religious value than the whole psalter said alone in one's cell; nevertheless, there must be times (as during Lent) of solitude and retirement. Theodosius sought to harmonize the contemplative and the active life, just as he sought to harmonize the needs of men as they are (and not as they ought to be) with the call to bring about the kingdom of God on earth. In these things he was following the Palestinian tradition and the spirit of St Basil.

Even when he had all the responsibility of ruling a large community and caring for the welfare of numerous spiritual children, St Theodosius still did his share of the ordinary daily work, whether in the fields or in the house; in particular he made it his business for two years to look after the needs of an old monk, Isaac, who was so infirm that he could neither sit up nor turn in his bed nor do anything for himself: Abbot Theodosius fed him, washed him, changed his clothes, did the least honourable offices for him—and then went out to sit at table with the grand-prince in the city. It is not surprising to read that his community was like a large family, 'where the young respected the old and the old were considerate to the young', where when one was at fault three or four were always at hand to share his penance. On the other hand it is clear that Theodosius had to wage ceaseless war on slackening discipline, and he was not always successful in his efforts.

A few short homilies and extracts from the sermons of St Theodosius have survived; they are full of biblical quotations and of a piece with the rest that is known about him. He had found St Antony's cave monastery 'narrow and depressing', and he sought spiritual as well as physical enlargement. 'Christ's love is overflowing upon us unworthy ones,' he said, and love must be met with love and it must flow beyond the cloister: 'Mindful of the word of the good Lord, my unworthy self declares to you that it is good for us to feed the hungry and the tramps with the fruits of our labour. . . If God's grace does not uphold and nourish us through the poor, what should we do with all our works?' He did not look on monks as a people apart, spiritual and corporal works of charity cannot be separated; and so equally, 'If I could, I would not let a day go by without throwing myself in tears at your feet and imploring you not to neglect a single hour of prayer.'

One of the most striking of the abbot's 'exhortations' was a single short sentence, a question he asked as he listened to the minstrels in Svyatoslav's hall: 'Sir, will you hear this music in the world to come?' The question showed he was conscious of the noxious effect that certain sorts of music can have on the human spirit, a consciousness that was lively in the Russian Church for hundreds of years. But he never overlooked that Jesus Christ is the light of a world that is beautiful as well as wicked. The likeness of St Theodosius to St Francis of Assisi, as well as their difference, is not difficult to see (Francis has a great appeal for Russian Christians): in either case gentleness, humbleness and patience are not characteristics attributed to them simply as hagiographical common-form. They loved Christ, who first loved us: 'What good have we done to him,' asked Theodosius, 'that he should choose us and deliver us from this transitory life? Have we not, all of us, gone astray and become useless for his service? . . . He sought us out, found us, carried us on his shoulders, and set us at the Father's right hand. Is he not the merciful lover of mankind? It was not we who sought him, but he us.'

During the Lent of 1074 St Theodosius had an intimation that his hour of release was at hand ('death is repose for the righteous,' observes his biographer). A day or two after Easter he was taken ill, and he told the brethren to choose a new abbot, for he would be leaving them on Saturday at sunrise. Then he asked to be left alone. But one of the monks peeped through the door, and saw his abbot face downwards on the floor and heard him imploring the prayers of the Mother of God and all the saints for himself and his flock. Then he got back into bed, and after a time a radiant smile appeared on his face; as if in recognition of some heavenly communication, 'Blessed be God!' he exclaimed. 'If it be so, I have no more fear and I leave this world happily.' Those were his last words.

In accordance with his express wish, St Theodosius was buried in one of the caves that formed the original monastery, but in 1091 his body was translated to the principal church and in 1108 he was canonized by the bishops of the Kiev province—the first of the *prepodobny*, 'very-like ones', that is, Christlike monks.

Of the monasteries built with the wealth of the princes of the house of Rurik and their nobles not a trace remains: they were all overshadowed in pre-Mongol Russia by the *laura* that began with the prayer and fasting of St Antony. The monastery of the Caves was devastated by the Tartars in 1240, in 1299 and again in 1316, and each time it recovered to take its place at the head of Russian monasteries and as one of the chief places of pilgrimage in the country, though never again did it touch the level of Christian life that it attained under the guidance of St Theodosius: it became too wealthy in this world's goods. Somewhere about its nine-hundredth birthday revolutionary fury appeared to bring this great house of God to an end, but in recent years it has been allowed to reopen.

The feast of St Theodosius (May 3) and of St Antony (July 10) are kept by Slavs of the Byzantine rite, both Catholic and Orthodox, and they are named in the preparation of the eucharistic Liturgy.

ST SAVA NEMANYA
Patron Saint of the Serbs

In the wild country between Jerusalem and the Dead Sea there is a famous monastery, one of the oldest occupied monasteries in the world, now known as Mar Saba, after the great Cappadocian St Sabas, who founded it in the year 483. His name became popular in the East, both to be given at baptism and when a man was clothed with the monastic habit, and among the later bearers of it none was more famous than the St Sabas who was the first archbishop of the Serbian church: in its Slavonic form of Sava he made the name an equal favourite in south-central Europe, for he is looked on, by Catholics and Orthodox alike, as *Prosvtitely*, 'the Enlightener', the spiritual founder and patron saint of the Serbian kingdom.

That kingdom took shape through the activity of the *megazupan* Stephen I Nemanya, between 1159 and 1195, and was formed by the union of two distinct and differing territories: the exclusively Serbian Rascia, whose capital was near the present Novi Pazar, and Primoria, whose capital was Duklya, near the present Podgoritsa in Montenegro, where the Serbs were not much more than a governing military minority. The Serbs, a Slav people from the land between the Carpathian mountains and the river Dniester, had established themselves in Rascia and neighbouring parts during the sixth and seventh centuries; missionaries were sent to them from Rome, apparently without much success, and their definitive conversion to Christianity was effected from Constantinople during the ninth century and after. The indigenous people of Primoria, on the other hand, were Illyrian by origin and Latin by religious rite. At this time there was a state of semi-separation between the Roman and the Byzantine churches; ecclesiastical allegiance was often a matter of politics, and Nemanya's secular interests lay away from Constantinople; it is accordingly found that he was, at the least, amicably disposed towards Old Rome.

Stephen I, founder of the dynasty of the Nemanydes, had three sons, Vukan, Stephen and Rastko, the youngest, who was born about 1176. The first two were characteristic young princes of the time and place (of most times and places): ambitious, quarrelsome, not too scrupulous, whose religion was easily overcome by passion. Rastko was different: he did not find it necessary to rush about noisily in order to get things done or to do everything with a crowd of other people, but he did find it necessary to learn to read and write, and he liked to be alone sometimes. One day when he was sixteen a Russian monk came to the Nemanya palace, begging for his monastery, and nobody was very surprised when it was found the next morning that the monk had gone and young Rastko with him.

He turned up again at Mount Athos, where he was given the habit and the name of Sava at the Russian monastery of St Pantaleimon (Roussiko; it still exists); from there he migrated to the neighbouring Greek house of Vatopedi. He was full of enthusiasm for his new life and wanted to begin at the end and be a hermit straight away: naturally the abbot would not allow this to a neophyte, but as a favour let him carry round the sack of bread when food was distributed to the various Vatopedi hermitages—an extremely exhausting job on a hot day, for some of the solitaries lived in almost inaccessible places on the Holy Mountain. 'Now,' he said, 'I know what I have always longed for—to reject the world and cling only to God.'

Sava kept in touch with his family, and when his father resigned his throne and himself became a monk, in 1196, he induced him to leave the monastery that he had founded at Studenitsa and come to Athos. Stephen (now the monk Simeon) arrived well-provided with this world's goods, and they were devoted to a work that was very near Sava's heart; namely, the foundation of an Athonite house for Serbian monks: the monastery, Khilandari, still exists as one of the twenty 'ruling monasteries' of the Holy Mountain, and, unlike once Georgian Iviron, it has not come into the hands of the Greeks. Here, when the thirteenth century was six weeks old, the first king of Serbia died, lying on a mat on the floor, a stone for his pillow.

Sava remained on Athos for another seven years. He was now abbot, and noted for his light and effective touch in training young monks; it was remarked, too, that his influence was always on the side of gentleness and leniency. He solidly established Khilandari and another foundation, drew up the necessary constitutions, and translated a number of books into his own language: among them was a psalter and ritual which is still in existence, written out by himself and signed: 'I, the unworthy lazy monk Sava.' But he also kept his eye on events at home, and they were not encouraging. At his retirement Stephen I had confided the government of Rascia to his son Stephen and of Primoria to Vukan, and the brothers had soon started to quarrel, the one calling on the Bulgars for help and the other on the Hungarians. This had a desolating effect on the kingdom, and the time came when the two princes made a truce of exhaustion and appealed to their younger brother to come home and help clear up the mess. In 1207 Sava left Mount Athos, taking with him the bones of his father to be enshrined at Studenitsa, where his memory is revered as that of a saint.

St Sava knew, what probably his brothers did not, that material prosperity and military success alone were not sufficient to bring peace and civilization to the Serbians and glory to the family of Nemanya: there was required as well a community of life, of ideas and of transcendental values that only religion could give. The Serbs had for some time been Christians, but much of it was a nominal Christianity, uninstructed and mixed up with relics of heathenism. It was the clergy's fault, but the clergy were not to blame: they were far too few, mostly uneducated, and materially not properly provided for. In the whole of Rascia (roughly modern Serbia) there was only one bishop, and he was subject to the Greek archbishop of Okhrida in Bulgaria—and that was the source of the trouble: the Greek clergy would not trouble themselves about these Slav barbarians who were dissociating themselves from the culture and civilization of the Byzantine empire (in which their function had been simply to pay taxes and provide soldiers). St Sava did a bold thing: following the example of the Benedictines in the West and against the general tradition of Eastern (especially Athonite) monasticism, he utilized the monks who had accompanied him from Khilandari for pastoral and missionary work among the people.

He established himself at Studenitsa (which lies north of Novi Pazar), from where he founded a number of small monasteries, settling them in places convenient for travelling around and getting at the people, rather than in those remote and breakneck spots so beloved of Eastern monks. But this did not mean that he had changed his mind about the necessity for spiritual health or facilities for solitude and contemplation: there may still be seen in the Studenitsa valley, high and away above the monastery, the rocky hermitage to which St Sava himself used to retire. 'Suddenly round the bend of a rock the hermitage comes into view. It consists of three buildings which must be very nearly unique. Two hundred feet from the top of the cliff were found three successive ledges about fifty yards long and never more than ten yards broad, from which there is a sheer drop of 1500 feet to the Studenitsa River, in flood time roaring below. On the uppermost ledge was built the chief hermitage glued to the rock, approachable only by a forty-foot ladder from the lower terrace. It reminds one of a swallow's nest and it looks as if the slightest tremor of the earth might send the whole structure crashing into the abyss.'[1]

Every people whose life has found a turning point in the religious activity of one man attribute to him in their gratitude other benefits for which he was only doubtfully responsible, if only because they are usually such simple things that their origins may well go back to prehistorical times: the men of Sussex, for example, say that St Wilfrid taught them how to catch fish. St Sava is no exception; the Serbian peasants say that before his time plowmen at the end of every furrow dragged their plow back to the starting point again instead of turning round across the top of the field, and cottages were lit and aired by leaving the door open instead of by making windows. A preacher could find some telling spiritual significances in those two things.

Stephen II was a good statesman, he saw the value of his brother's activities from a secular as well as a religious point of view, and he encouraged them in every way. But as a politician he was specially pleased when Sava decided that the time had come to get rid of the ecclesiastical over-

[1] Radmilo Vucić, in *Sobornost*, Summer, 1955.

lordship of Okhrida. It was a peculiarly favourable moment to do so: the Franks were in occupation of Constantinople and the Eastern emperor and the Oecumenical Patriarch in exile at Nicaea, so that the Byzantine church was in a state of confusion, added to which the metropolitan of Okhrida was in conflict with the patriarch. So to Nicaea Sava went. He won over the emperor, Theodore II Laskaris (who was related to the Nemanya family), to agree that the Serbian people should have their own hierarchy, and the emperor designated Sava as their first metropolitan. The patriarch, Manuel Kharitopoulos, disagreed but in the circumstances dared not oppose obstinately, and he consecrated Sava bishop in 1219. Sava returned home by way of Mount Athos, bringing with him more monks, and many books that had been translated at Khilandari. At once on his arrival he held a synod, at which Serbia was divided into a number of dioceses; in some of the western parts there were already Latin bishops, but the new hierarchy was exclusively concerned with the faithful of Byzantine rite.

The circumstances of the coronation as king of Stephen II, 'the First-Crowned', are very uncertain. One contemporary states that at Stephen's request a legate was sent from Rome, who crowned him in 1217. But it is also said that when St Sava returned from Nicaea he wrote to Pope Honorius III announcing his episcopal ordination and asking a royal crown from the shrine of the Apostles for his brother. The pope replied favourably, and in 1222 Sava crowned Stephen in the monastery church at Zicha. That there should in fact have been a double coronation is quite likely.

Thus, before he was fifty years old, the youth who had run away from home to be a monk had played a large part in consolidating the state founded by his father by providing for the healthy religious life of the people, giving them bishops of their own nationality, and ensuring the sovereign status of their ruler.

The twentieth-century reader may well be puzzled by the apparently equivocal position of Sava, King Stephen, and their people between the Holy See and Constantinople: Sava goes to the second for permission to set up a hierarchy and to receive episcopal orders, and then turns to the first with every expression of dutifulness to ask a crown for his brother. It must be understood, on the one hand, that in those days the rift between East and West had not yet hardened into definite, unambiguous separation; the West still regarded Constantinople as a patriarchate of the Universal Church, but temporarily estranged, rather than as a 'different church'. On the other hand, the rift had not yet penetrated the more remote provinces of the Byzantine church, and the Slavs, who from the Adriatic to the Black Sea had a certain 'national' sentiment in common, while familiar with the distinction between one and another rite of worship and ecclesiastical organization, did not yet know any division into Catholic and Orthodox. It was only right and proper that St Sava should go for a hierarchical organization to the competent authority of his patriarchate, and should then turn to the Supreme Pontiff for recognition of and blessing on the new state of affairs. Furthermore, behind the various ecclesiastical authorities concerned there were corresponding secular powers between which the new Serbian kingdom had to move with great care.

The Serbian Orthodox, revering St Sava as the founder of their national church, long took it for granted that he was never in communion with Rome, at any rate in any effective sense; and this created a somewhat embarrassing position for the Catholics of Yugoslavia. However, for some time now the cultus of the saint has lost its narrow and unhistorical 'denominational' character, under pressure both of political events and of learned research. During

1935, for example, anticipating the seventh centenary of his death, celebrations were held in his honour at Paris and an Orthodox Yugoslav, Professor Arnautović, demonstrated Sava's collaboration with neighbouring Latin bishops and his indubitable recognition of the Holy See; at Belgrade in the following year an address on 'St Sava, Monk and Bishop' was given by a Catholic priest, Father Privat Bélard, and his conclusions in the same sense were well received by the many distinguished Orthodox clergy and laymen present.[1]

The closing years of Sava's life were marked exteriorly by two voyages to Palestine and the Near East. The first, in 1229, seems to have been a pilgrimage of devotion: the second, in 1233, provides another example of that undefined ecclesiastical position to which reference has just been made. The church in eastern Bulgaria, with its primatial see at Trnovo, was then in unambiguous communion with Rome, but the tsar John Assen II wanted his independence of Constantinople recognized by the Oecumenical Patriarch: as a preliminary, therefore, he asked the archibishop of the Serbs to try and obtain the agreement of the other Orthodox patriarchs, Alexandria, Antioch and Jerusalem. St Sava accordingly set out with a large retinue, 'a veritable legate of the young Slav churches to the apostolic churches of the East'. He established a hospice for Serbian pilgrims at Jerusalem and made arrangements for the reception of Serbian monks in various great monasteries, including Mount Sinai, and

---

[1] The paper of Father Bélard is the source of most of this account of St Sava, who figures in the Bollandist *Acta Sanctorum* (Jan. 14) and in several Latin calendars of Illyria and Dalmatia, as well as in that of the Catholic Byzantine diocese of Krizevtsi. A Latin bishop of Bosnia, Ivan Tomko Mrnavić, wrote a life of him in the sixteenth century, and the Franciscan Andrew Kachić devoted one of his best poems to the saint.

fresco portrait, painted circa 1235 ; *Church of Mileshevo, Yugoslavia*

St Sava Nemanya

St Sava's summer Hermitage

arrived back in Trnovo towards the end of 1235. He had
a most enthusiastic reception, for his mission had been
successful.

But his fatiguing journeys and many activities had
affected his health, and he decided to stay for a while in
the Bulgarian city in order to rest and recuperate. John
Assen offered the use of his own palace, 'not only to do
Sava honour, but because it was well warmed and com-
fortable'. But instead of recovering he got worse, and it
became clear that he was nearing his end. The archbishop
of Trnovo called on him one day and found him so bad
that he wanted to fetch the tsar, but Sava would not hear
of it: 'No, no, good bishop: you must please not trouble
about me. Thank you for coming to see me. Now please
go back to your own house and leave me to myself and to
God.' During the night of 14 January 1236, St Sava received the body and blood of Christ and then, with a smile
on his face, died.

St Sava wanted only to be a monk, but another call came
and he answered it: 'For your sake, my people, I left the
sacred happiness of my retreat and returned to seek your
souls. If you listen to me and if God enables me to do good
among you, if you become holy and one in God, there will
be two-fold gain, and salvation will be ours.' He set before
his countrymen a high ideal of Christian religion and life,
and provided for the local organization of the Church
divinely founded for the incorporation of all mankind,
collectively and individually, in Jesus Christ. The *Life of
St Simeon* that he wrote had a strong influence on early
Serbian historical and biographical writing, and he
directed the translation from Greek of the country's first
written code of law. In these and other ways Sava was
indeed the father-in-God of his people.

The body of the saint was buried at the monastery of
Milochevo in Serbia, where it reposed until 1594. In that

year there was an insurrection of Serbs in Banat, and the Turks sent Sinan Pasha, an Italian renegade to Islam, to suppress it; morally to terrorize the rebels, he seized the revered relics of St Sava and publicly burnt them upon a hill above Belgrade.

THE VENERABLE MEKHITAR
OF SIVAS
Abbot

At the end of the fifth century the Church of Armenia formally rejected the Council of Chalcedon, and ever since then has been counted among the monophysite churches, in communion neither with Catholics nor Orthodox. From time to time, and under various influences, numbers of Armenians (who from early ages have had 'colonies' in many parts of the world) have been reconciled with Rome; and during the seventeenth century Constantinople became the great Catholic Armenian centre. For some years after 1695 they were seriously persecuted at the instigation of some of their dissident brethren, among the victims being the priest Gomidas Keumurgian, who was beatified as a martyr in 1929.

At this time one of the most promising of the Armenian clergy was Father Mekhitar, who had been born at Sivas (the ancient Sebastea) in Asia Minor in 1670, his father being a merchant of some consideration. The boy was christened Manugh ('child') and he did not receive the name Mekhitar ('consoler'), by which he is commonly known, until his ordination to the diaconate. From the age of five to ten he received the rudiments of education from a priest and was then turned over to the care of two girls who led a semi-eremitical life with their mother, and their chaplain cultivated the boy's taste for learning. Manugh was intended to go into his father's business, but the influence of this household confirmed his own inclination and at the age of fifteen, after a deal of opposition, he got his father's permission to become a monk.

Armenian monks had by the seventeenth century become practically celibate secular priests, many of them vartapets,[1] living in community but often leaving their monasteries to preach or study or simply to travel or collect alms. They conserved after a fashion the learning and culture of the Armenian nation but were by no means always worthy or learned, and the monasteries were apt to be centres from which the separation from Rome was strengthened and encouraged. At this period it was often difficult to tell whether individual Armenians were in schism or not, but Manugh belonged to a family which seems to have been in at least implicit communion with the Catholic Church. The monastery he chose to go to was that of Holy Cross, near Sivas, and he was ordained deacon at once by the abbot-bishop on the recommendation of his tutor. But he did not find Holy Cross a satisfactory place, he saw no prospect of increasing either in knowledge or virtue there, and at the end of the same year, 1691, he set out for Etshmiadzin, the seat of the chief bishop of the Armenians and the intellectual centre of their church. On the way, at Erzerum, he for the first time met a priest of the Western church, a Jesuit, and from his conversation gained a strong desire to visit Rome.

Mekhitar's two months' stay at Etshmiadzin was very unhappy. It was terribly cold in the mountains, he was tired and ill, and the prelate to whom he had attached himself treated him with scant consideration or sympathy. So he went back to Erzerum, visiting various shrines on the way, and, after a short stay at the monastery of Bassen,

---

[1] The office of *vartapet* is a rank of the clergy peculiar to the Armenians, specially authorized to preach and teach.

returned to Holy Cross in the summer of 1693. Though suffering from some affliction of the eyes which for a time blinded him, he passed the next twelve months in quiet study; at this time he wrote a hymn, both words and melody, in honour of our Lady which is still sung among Armenians. Then the abbot was superseded by another superior, under whose misrule the monastery lost what little discipline it had, and Mekhitar resolved to leave altogether. He would go to Rome.

But the time was not yet. He stayed three months in Aleppo where, after prolonged discussion with the local Jesuit fathers, he made a formal profession of Catholic faith, and then continued his voyage. At Cyprus, however, he was struck down by malaria, and after suffering for two months was still so weak that there was nothing for him to do but to go back home.

In the spring of 1696 Mekhitar was ordained priest and, though still only twenty, he now turned his mind to the possibility of a religious congregation which by preaching and teaching should revive the spirit of Christ among the Armenian people and restore formal union of the whole church with the Catholic West, so putting an end to the uncertainty and particularism that was so damaging to their religious and intellectual welfare. Accordingly he went to Constantinople to discuss his ideas with the vartapet Khatchatur, of whose wisdom and goodness he had heard a great deal. Khatchatur had been trained in Rome, and had acquired the leisurely Roman prudence and the Western addiction to what the English call 'red tape'. He listened patiently and kindly to what Mekhitar had to say, then shook his head and said firmly that he would have nothing to do with it: Mekhitar, he pointed out, was too young, he had no experience of ecclesiastical organization, above all, he had no money.

During five months in Constantinople Mekhitar made

a name for himself as a preacher at the church of St Gregory the Enlightener at Galata, but he failed to make Father Khatchatur change his mind. So he resolved to go east, away from the enervating influence of the great city, and see if he could get support there. Accompanied by two young men, both named John, one of whom had followed him from Sivas, he went by the Black Sea to Samsun, walked south-east, preaching amid great enthusiasm at the Armenian centres he passed through, and arrived at the monastery called Karmir Vank, fifteen miles from Erzerum. He was well received by the abbot-bishop Makar, who put him in charge of the studies of the young clerics and at the end of a year invested him with the teaching staff of a vartapet.

Mekhitar took this opportunity to make known to the bishop his scheme for a religious congregation, and to ask if he would not himself take the leadership of the work. This Makar would not do, but he approved of it and made no objection to two of his community, Father Gabriel and Father Lazarus, joining Father Mekhitar. So, with these two and John of Sivas, he left Karmir Vank and went to Erzerum, the civil capital of Armenia, where he intended to make a final effort to get support and help. He was well received by the people and earned golden opinions from several Latin religious that he met there, but he inevitably fell foul of the bishop, Avedik, a man notorious as a persecutor, and after some months Mekhitar came to the conclusion that he was wasting his time in Armenia. By July 1700 he was back again at Constantinople.

He found the Armenian community in the city turned upside down by persecution of the unionist party and he worked tirelessly to form a common mind among his fellow countrymen. His followers now numbered eight and, lest so relatively large a concentration should provoke the suspicion of the dissident patriarch, he sent three of them to preach in Armenia. With the remainder he began that work that was to be so characteristic of his monks in after years, printing and publishing: the first book issued was an Armenian version of the *Imitation of Christ*. But scarcely was the infant community established secretly in a house at Pera than persecution of Catholics became chronic under the patriarch Ephrem, and the leading clergy had to go into hiding. Mekhitar's refuge was at the Capuchin friary (on his way thither he passed a soldier sent to arrest him but, like St Athanasius of Alexandria in somewhat similar circumstances, he was not recognized), and he had seriously to consider what was to be done next: it was obviously impossible to found and make effective a religious community in circumstances such as then obtained at Constantinople. He thought of the Lebanon, that secular refuge of oppressed Christians, but eventually decided in favour of the Morea peninsula in Greece, because many Armenian merchants traded there, it was not far from the principal Armenian centres, and it was since 1687 under the rule of the Venetian Republic. Once his mind was made up he acted thoroughly and promptly: having received an assurance from the Venetian ambassador that his monks would be welcome, he recalled the missionaries from Armenia, sent two monks on in advance to prepare a place, got the others out of Constantinople by ones and twos, and finally himself escaped to Smyrna, whence he reached Nauplia in February 1703. When the fugitives were at last all gathered together they numbered twelve priests and three aspirants, not including the bishop Hovnan, an old friend of Mekhitar, who had accompanied them but was not a member of the community.

The newcomers were most generously welcomed. The Venetian authorities made them a grant of land and a house at Modon, on the coast, together with a village and a half as part endowment, on condition that the monks should build a proper monastery within three years. Common life was at once begun and the four seniors made their religious profession, according to the Rule of St Antony, with a vow to undertake mission work added. In the autumn of 1705 Fathers Elias and John were sent to Rome to submit the community's constitutions to the Holy See. Meanwhile recruits had been coming in steadily, and several missioners were sent out to Turkey and Asia Minor.

But these early days were far from being without difficulties. There was opposition to the new congregation (there always is), and there were grave financial embarrassments due to the fact that Mekhitar had to borrow money in order to fulfil his undertaking to build a monastery. That obligation, and indeed necessity, was duly discharged and the church was consecrated by the Latin archbishop of Corinth. The principal objections raised against Mekhitar's undertaking were that he acted too independently of the ecclesiastical authorities, that his missioners were ignorant men, and that they had far too high an opinion of their leader.[1] He was able to demonstrate the falsity of these and other charges and at last, in 1711, the Holy See gave its approval of the new congregation, but on condition that its monastic life should be based on one of three rules, Basil's, Benedict's or Augustine's. That of St Benedict was unanimously chosen 'as being known to us Armenians for many centuries' (it had first been translated by St Nerses of Lambron in the twelfth) and, though the Holy Rule was modified somewhat to meet their special requirements, the Mekhitarists are reckoned part of the Benedictine family, though outside the general Western confederation.

From the first Abbot Mekhitar was a firm upholder not only of the Armenian rites of worship and religious

---

[1] That he was, in fact, literally inspired by the Holy Ghost—and could transmit his inspiration to his followers.

customs but also of giving a prominent place in studies and preaching to the teaching of the Armenian fathers and divines of the past. This upset those Armenian clergy who, having undergone a Western training at the Urban College of Propaganda and elsewhere, had accepted the methods of the later developments of the medieval Friars of Unity[1] and got the idea that only Latin theologians could be really orthodox and only Latin observances fully Catholic. Owing to the slanders of the less scrupulous of this party, the abbot had to recall one of his best subjects, Father Elias, from his work at Constantinople—ironically enough, Mekhitar was at the time engaged with Father John of Sivas in translating the *Summa Theologica* of St Thomas into Armenian.[2]

By 1714 the money troubles of the monastery were pretty well over and the outlook for the future was good, when war began to threaten between the Venetians and the Turks. Mekhitar knew the strength of the Turkish arms, and he knew that the Morea would be their first objective: he realized that the whole of his work was in danger. He therefore decided at once to provide a place of refuge in case of need and, leaving half a dozen monks in charge at Modon, he departed with the rest of the community,

---

[1] They represented an attempt to combine Eastern monasticism with the rule of the Dominicans, but became to all intents and purposes a Western order with an Armenian exterior.

[2] This trouble persisted. The following is an extract from a letter written to the Holy See in 1816 by Mgr. Coressi, Latin vicar apostolic at Constantinople: 'All these differences between [the Mekhitarists] and the secular clergy arise from the fact that the first wish to be Catholic and Armenian too, while the second want to be Catholic and Latin—or pseudo-Latin. . . The truth is that the methods of the Mekhitarists greatly help in the conversion of schismatical and heretical Armenians, while the methods of the others only serve to flatter us, the Latin bishop and clergy. It is surely right to prefer the unalloyed good of the conversion of souls rather than the less pure good of our own interests and utility.'

eleven in number, to Venice. Doubtless he was criticized for 'panicking', but the abbot knew what he was doing, and events proved him right. War was declared on 3 December 1714: within a few weeks Corinth and Nauplia had fallen, and at the beginning of August the Turks took Modon by assault. There was a general massacre of Christians, and the Armenian monastery was sacked and gutted along with the other chief buildings of the town. With the help of merchants the monks managed to escape, and eventually after great hardships joined their fellows at Venice.

Materially and administratively Abbot Mekhitar had now to start all over again, but he had used admirable foresight in choosing Venice. There were at that time a score and more Armenian colonies in Italy, dating from the thirteenth and fourteenth centuries; Venice was the chief of them,[1] and the priest of the Armenian church there was now that vartapet Khatchatur whom we have already met in Constantinople trying to discourage the enthusiasm of the young Mekhitar. His doubts had been falsified in an unmistakable way, and he took the lead in encouraging the local nobility and clergy to help the refugee monks. On 26 August 1717, the Most Serene Republic agreed to rent to 'the Armenian Fathers of St Antony the Abbot' the island of San Lazzaro, which lies between the Guidecca and (what mercifully for the monks was not yet a European resort) the Lido.

There was a disused church and some empty buildings on the island, but while the monks were reducing the place to order and making it habitable their abbot's attention was distracted to a very different matter. The opponents of his congregation had not ceased to be active and he had been instructed by the Holy See to recall two of his missioners, Fathers George and Joseph, from the East to answer

[1] The first Armenian printed book was published in Venice in 1513; it was a work on astrology.

charges that were laid against them. When they arrived he set out with Father George and another, and reached Rome in June 1718, twenty-five years after his first attempt to go there. He found that the charges against his monks were those that have already been mentioned, and in addition that they preached and heard confessions without authorization and used their missionary journeys as an occasion to collect alms for their community. Mekhitar, who was armed with glowing testimonials from Latin prelates and religious both in Europe and Asia Minor, answered the accusations, and after a stay of four months in Rome a plenary assembly of cardinals dismissed all the charges and fully justified the Mekhitarists both collectively and individually.[1]

Arising out of this inquiry were certain questions about the sort of 'intercommunion' that existed between Catholic and other Armenians in the Turkish dominions. This was a common state of affairs in the Near East in the seventeenth and eighteenth centuries. Catholics and dissidents were mixed up in the same congregations, a church would have a dissident pastor at one time and a Catholic at another; Jesuits and Capuchins were invited to preach and hear confessions by Orthodox, Armenian and other bishops in their churches, and did so. Mekhitar and the vartapet Khatchatur gave considered opinions to Cardinal Tanara that these practices were justified and required in the circumstances, and the pope (Clement XI) ordered that the matter should be further inquired into. The controversy was ended only in 1729 when, conditions having changed and been alleviated, the Holy See forbade Catholic Armenians any longer to frequent dissident churches. But

---

[1] It appears that the charge of ignorance was simply based on the fact that they had not studied at the Urban College of Propaganda. And it was proved that Mekhitar had forbidden his missioners to solicit or *to accept* alms, a rule they had obeyed.

before this happened the business was an occasion of much distress to Mekhitar, because he was represented by some as interpreting Clement XI's decree as meaning that Catholics could meanwhile *freely* and as it were wantonly receive sacraments from the hands of non-Catholics. This misrepresentation did not survive an excellent letter that he addressed to the Holy See in 1721, in which he reconciled the current practice with orthodox Catholic teaching.

Meanwhile the monastery of San Lazzaro was prospering. The religious spirit of the house was excellent and missioners were sent to the old Armenian colonies in Poland and Transylvania as well as to Turkey, Asia Minor and Mesopotamia. Love of God and his gospel was what Mekhitar sent them to preach; they were to help those in need, freely to forgive every slight or wrong suffered, to be humble, gentle and unacquisitive: 'the monk should return to his monastery as poor as he left it.' At the same time the intellectual work of the monks was leading to nothing less than a literary renaissance among the whole Armenian people: their scientific,[1] literary and religious studies, and the printing and diffusion of books which went (and still go) throughout the world, conserved the Armenian tongue as a living language at a time when it was threatened with extinction. Books were published from 1719 onwards and ten years later Mekhitar bought the famous printing-press of the vartapet Oskan in Amsterdam and set it up at Venice. The principal of the personal contributions of the abbot to this work were his grammars of classical and vernacular Armenian, an Armenian dictionary, a catechism, commentaries on St Matthew's gospel and other books, work on the great vernacular Bible of 1735, and translations of the *Summae* of St Thomas, of the *Summa* of St

---

[1] It appears that some ingenious young monks constructed a device such as that which in the West takes its name from the Earl of *Orrery*, without ever having seen or heard of his.

Albert the Great, and of the *Paradisus Animae* attributed to the last-named—a marvellous record of scholarship for a man who had so many responsibilities on his shoulders. He had, too, considerable talent as an architect. He had designed the first monastery at Modon himself, and to crown his work at San Lazzaro he planned and carried out a rebuilding of the church and cells, and added refectory, novitiate, guest quarters, in fact a whole large airy monastery, built after the fashion of the time and place, but plain and not too exuberantly decorated, in accordance with its monastic purpose.

During the last three years of his life Abbot Mekhitar suffered from serious ill-health, which abated his energy only when it forced him to bed. The end came in his seventy-fourth year, and he died among his brethren on 27 April 1749. His courage, determination and faith are shown in the history of the foundation of his order, and the sort of man he was is shown by the sort of order he founded. The spirit that he commended to his missioners is an index to his own, and the uninterrupted stream of pilgrims to his tomb at San Lazzaro witnesses to the conviction that he was a Christian of heroic stature; the process for his beatification is in progress. Veneration for the memory of Abbot Mekhitar is by no means confined to his Catholic fellow countrymen, for others have benefited almost as much from the work of the order he founded. For example, at the bicentenary of their foundation in 1901, the dissident katholikos at Etshmiadzin, Baptist Krimian, chief hierarch of the Armenian nation, recognized its achievements by sending to the monastery at Venice a copy of the picture called 'Our Lady of Sevan', in contemplation of which Mekhitar had once, it is said, experienced a vision of the Mother of God. It was the wish of the katholikos to send the original picture, but he was overruled.

In our day the Mekhitarist monks continue the life and

work mapped out for them by their founder. A separate branch was established in 1773, first at Trieste and then at Vienna, and the monasteries of Venice and Vienna now have together over a hundred monks, three-quarters of whom are priests. Each house has its polyglot press, with colleges, schools, missions and other works for Armenians in France, Italy, Greece, Turkey, Egypt and Lebanon.

The Mekhitarist press at San Lazzaro is pretty well known but not so well known as it ought to be, and the following particulars of some of its activities are in place: The first books published there were two devotional works in 1719, and these were followed (among others) by the New Testament (1720), an illustrated translation of the Bible (1735), Mekhitar's commentary on St Matthew's Gospel (1737) and his grammar and dictionary (1749). Given to the Armenian people by the press in the course of two hundred years are works of St Thomas Aquinas and of many of the fathers, both Eastern and Western; the *Iliad* and the *Odyssey*, a complete Virgil, the dialogues of Plato, the tragedies of Sophocles, Cicero's *De officiis*, Plutarch's *Lives*, the *Annales* of Tacitus, Thucydides on the Peloponnesian war, the *Ars poetica* of Horace, and writings of Euripides, Julius Caesar, Seneca, Sallust and Marcus Aurelius, as well as the whole of the *Divine Comedy*. Among the original works published have been several biblical commentaries, numerous treatises of biography and history, geography, mathematics and physics, poetry and rhetoric, law, medicine, dictionaries and grammars, a world atlas, volumes of poems, and numerous books dealing with Armenia and its people. The monks recovered from Armenian sources and published commentaries on Tatian's *Diatessaron* and on St Paul's epistles by St Ephrem the Syrian (1836, 1893), the works of the katholikos John IV the Philosopher (1834), two treatises and a commentary of Philo Judaeus (1822, 1827) and the edition of the *Chronicle* of Eusebius edited by Father J. B. Aucher and Cardinal Mai, in 1818. Among the translations of more modern works are the funeral sermons of Bossuet, several books of Fénelon, the *Polyeucte* of Corneille, Buffon's *Birds*, selected poems of Leopardi, Byron[1] and 'Carmen Sylva', *Paradise Lost*, *The Deserted Village*, Young's *Night Thoughts*, Macpherson's *Ossian* and— *Uncle Tom's Cabin*.

The 1960 catalogue of the publications of this press contains 100 closely printed crown 8vo pages of Armenian books published since 1716, of which many, of course, are out of print. The section of works in Latin and other European languages includes thirty-four items in English, or giving English texts, apparently still in print. A small volume called *Preces Sancti Nersetis* (10th ed. 1882) is a good example of the technical skill of the Mekhitarist printers. It consists of twenty-four short prayers of St Nerses Glaietsi in thirty-six different languages, including Irish, Greenlandic, Icelandic, Malayalam, Serbian, Turkish, Chinese, Hebrew and Ethiopic. It involves the use of fifteen alphabets of characters besides the Roman.

---

[1] Like so many people on the continent the Armenians rate Byron as a poet very high indeed; but this may not be due exclusively to his poetry. His name is one of the earliest in the visitors' book at San Lazzaro, and he was a welcome visitor there. Cf. his letter from Venice to Augusta Leigh, dated 18 December 1816, and others.

BLESSED GABRA MICHAEL
Martyr

The land of Ethiopia, more often but less properly called
Abyssinia, first heard the good news of Christ somewhere
about the year 330 from two young Tyrian men, Frumentius and Aedesius, in circumstances which are reported,
correctly or not, by Rufinus; it is certain that St Frumentius
was consecrated bishop by St Athanasius at Alexandria
and fixed his see at Aksum about the middle of the fourth
century. More extensive evangelization was carried on by
the Nine Saints, who were probably Syrian monophysites,
and the hierarchical dependence on the Church of Egypt
caused Ethiopia to follow her in the definite choice of
Monophysism (cf. page 80). Then came the Arab con-
quest of Egypt, and for nine hundred years Ethiopia was
practically entirely cut off from contact with orthodox
Christendom. Relations were established with the trading
and adventuring Portuguese at the beginning of the sixteenth century, and in 1555 Pope Julius III appointed a
'patriarch of Ethiopia', but this is not the place to retell
that sad story: it is sufficient to say that in 1622 the negus[1]
Susneyos proclaimed union with Rome for the whole of
his kingdom, and that ten years later his successor pro-
scribed Catholicism and drove every European Catholic
beyond the frontier. For two hundred years Ethiopia was

[1] The word *negus* does not mean 'emperor' but 'king'. *Negus
neghesti*, 'king of kings', is the title of the Ethiopic sovereign.

closed to Catholic priests, and those who tried to enter the country generally lost their lives in the attempt: in 1638 a Jesuit, Apollinaris de Almeida, and the beatified Capuchins, Agathangelo and Cassian, were martyred; three Friars Minor were massacred at Suakim in 1650, and three more (one an Ethiopian in origin) at Massawa in 1671; some French Jesuits were killed at the beginning of the eighteenth century, three Capuchins and others were stoned to death in 1711, Father Antony of Rivaralo and two others were sent into slavery at Socotra in 1725, and Father Ignatius Ballerini was killed in 1797.

The work of again making a permanent Catholic settlement in Ethiopia was reserved to Father Justin de Jacobis, a Lazarist from Naples, and the way was opened for him by the Irish-French traveller A. T. d'Abbadie d'Arrast, who induced Pope Gregory XVI in 1839 to set up a prefecture apostolic at Adowa. It was put in charge of Lazarists, with Father Justin at their head, and it was not long before he made the acquaintance of an Ethiopian monk named Gabra Michael (i.e., servant of St Michael; *Gabra Mika'el*).

This man had been born about 1790 at Mertola Mariam in the province of Gojjam, of parents who probably had some Portuguese blood in their veins; showing an appetite and aptitude for study, he was sent to school when he was ten in a local monastery. The Church of Ethiopia was a mixture of religion and superstition in which the simple goodness and austerity of the few was swamped in the ignorance and vice of the many; their priesthood was most insufficient, almost wholly untrained and commanding little respect among the people: nor is this surprising, seeing how long Ethiopia had been hemmed in by Islam and predatory European powers and in only difficult contact even with the oppressed Christians of Egypt. Much of the consistent Christianity and all the learning (it consisted largely in extravagant theological speculation) that there was in the Ethiopian church was to be found among the monks, of whom there was a huge number. They were held in considerable esteem by the people, but were far from being always worthy of it, for there were so many of them and their life so loosely controlled (or not at all) that their standard was exceedingly uneven. Many were wanderers, some hermits, and the common life of those who did live in community was very sketchy. Antony d'Abbadie, who knew them well, had a high opinion of the better sort of monk: 'Some of them,' he wrote, 'seem in a measure to have regained the majestic security of primeval man moving in a sphere out of the reach of evil, and it is easy to understand how the respect and admiration they evoke may make you think you see a sort of halo floating round their peaceful faces.' Such a one in time became Gabra Michael.

He studied assiduously, supporting himself according to custom by begging food in the neighbouring villages, and at the age of seventeen he received the title of *alaka*, which qualified him for ecclesiastical administrative posts in temporal affairs. But he stayed on at the monastery, where he soon found that his discontent with the spiritual state of his church was extending to its theology: for example, the Monophysism which it professed was understood in at least four different ways by the quarrelsome theologians. By the time he was twenty-five Gabra Michael was a 'professed' monk (but not a priest—few oriental monks are priests), and he became so respected by the community at Mertola Mariam that after some years it was suggested he should reform the monastery in accordance with the classical *Book of Monks*.[1] There was no copy

---

[1] I have tried in vain to get any certain information about this work. The best suggestion seems to be that it may have been one of the collections of *Apophthegmata Patrum*, sayings and anecdotes of the

of this theoretically indispensable work at Mertola, and Gabra Michael was sent to borrow one from the monks of Debra Motsa; they could not find one either, so he took the staff and gourd of a pilgrim and set out to look for one.

He wandered from monastery to monastery, joining in interminable theological arguments but looking in vain for any fruitful monastic life or any copy of the *Book of Monks*. At length he came in 1829 to Gondar, then the chief city of Ethiopia, and here at last he found what he was after: he betook himself to a learned teacher named Walda Selassie, who expounded to him the life and teaching of the precious book. But Gabra Michael did not then return to Mertola Mariam or any of the other monasteries that stood so badly in need of his knowledge and good will; he stopped on at Gondar, sitting at the feet of Walda Selassie. And in time he became himself a teacher, having his own disciples (among them a young nobleman named John) and making his own (orthodox) contribution to the vexed question of the human nature of Christ—whereupon the monks of Ennefsiah charged him with Arianism. For eleven years he lived in the capital before he came to the conclusion that he would never find the answers to his doubts and questionings within the limits of his own land; his mind turned towards Jerusalem: where could the faith of the primitive Church be found if not in the city where Jesus Christ had redeemed the world?

Gabra Michael was now about fifty, but he set out on his travels again. At Debra Damo the monks cursed him

---

early monks and hermits. Such a collection is extant in Coptic, though not, so far as is known, in Ethiopic. I am indebted for this suggestion to Dr De Lacy O'Leary. Professor O. H. E. Burmester, of Cairo, tells me there is an Ethiopic version of the *Paradise of the Egyptian Fathers*.

as a heretic and threatened to throw him from the cliff on which their house was perched, and at Gunde Gunde he talked long with a young monk named Takla Haymanot (after a great thirteenth-century bishop) whom he was to meet again in very different circumstances; at length he reached the port of Massawa on the Red Sea. How he was going to get to Jerusalem he did not know, but he learned that a delegation was getting ready to go to Cairo to ask the Coptic patriarch to do his duty by appointing a bishop for Ethiopia, whose only see he had left vacant for twenty years. Gabra Michael got himself attached to the Tigrai delegation, and then learned that they were to travel under the protection of a European—none other than Father de Jacobis, who had agreed to undertake the responsibility provided that the delegation were also accredited to the Holy See.

During the journey Gabra Michael was impressed by the dignified and modest bearing of the Neapolitan priest in face of the rudeness of some of his companions, but what conversation may have passed between the two is not known. They arrived at Cairo in the spring of 1841, and the patriarch Peter put forward as a suitable *abuna*[1] for Ethiopia a young priest named Andrew, who had had some education in a Protestant mission school but had till recently been a camel-driver. Gabra Michael protested, but the other five delegates agreed, under pressure, and Abba Andrew was consecrated, taking the name of Salama. A few days later the patriarch was asked his views on the theological problems that troubled the Ethiopians. He indicated Salama: 'There is your shepherd,' he said. But the shepherd remained silent, seeming to have no views on the subject.

'If you don't know anything about these things, what

[1] *Abuna*, 'our father', the title of the chief bishop of the Ethiopian church.

are you going to do when you get to our country?' asked Gabra Michael pertinently.

'You're a blind old fool',[1] or words to that effect, retorted Salama, and Gabra Michael was heard to murmur that he feared the new bishop was blind in spirit. Salama neither forgot nor forgave.

The patriarch made a feeble attempt to stop the Ethiopians from going on to Rome, but Father de Jacobis held them to it. They were received by Pope Gregory XVI and assisted at the Holy Mysteries in St Peter's on the feast of the Assumption. Gabra Michael was very impressed by what he saw, and by what he was told of Catholic doctrine concerning the natures of our Lord; indeed, he was convinced that that was the true Christian doctrine, but he was not yet prepared to separate himself from the church of his countrymen. Father de Jacobis then escorted them to Palestine, where at Jaffa one of the delegates was taken seriously ill, made his profession of Catholic faith, received the last sacraments, and recovered; and so, by 'the way of the land of the Philistines', they got back to Cairo.

The leader of the delegation, who had been very reserved and on his guard in Rome, now told the Coptic patriarch that, 'If you love your neighbour as the gospel says, you will set an example by becoming a Catholic' (it is not recorded that he followed his own advice). Gabra Michael was less rhetorical and absolute. He had been looking for the truth about the God-man; he had found it, not as he had expected at Jerusalem, where he found every church a sect, but at Rome; and now he was concerned to convey that truth to those who were in error. He got up before the patriarchal synod and called on the patriarch to issue an order to Abuna Salama forbidding him to teach that our Lord's Godhead absorbed and nullified his man-

[1] Gabra Michael was in fact blind in one eye.

hood.[1] It was done, and the following rider was added, 'But do not allow any Catholic church to be opened, for if you do your country will be flooded out by foreigners'. To this addition Gabra Michael raised no objection.

At this time his one idea was the total restoration of the church of his people by acceptance of the true doctrine about Christ, which would lead to a better understanding of his teaching and what it demanded of them; moreover, once their faith was orthodox there would be no grounds for interference by Christians from outside. He had no illusions about the difficulty of the task, and before entering on it he spent some time in retirement with Father de Jacobis. Meanwhile a thing favourable to his cause had come to pass: his former pupil John (Attieh Yohannes) had come to the throne at Gondar, and in the winter of 1842-43 Gabra Michael betook himself to that city.

King John and his chief minister, Ras Ali (who really ruled the kingdom), were quite ready to promulgate the Coptic patriarch's decree and Gabra Michael attended at the bishop's house to deliver it to Abuna Salama. That young man accepted the document and then, without reading it, stuffed it contemptuously away in his clothes: 'Get out!' he exclaimed. 'You are excommunicated!'

'You cannot excommunicate me,' replied the monk. 'If you ignore the patriarch's commands you have no jurisdiction over us.'

And King John agreed, even going so far as to order Salama to be put to death for his insubordination. But Gabra Michael intervened on his behalf and he was instead banished from Amhara. It looked as if orthodoxy were going to triumph, but this momentary appearance was the extent of Gabra Michael's success. The interference of the Coptic patriarch in what the Ethiopians regarded as their

---

[1] It was expressed in the terms of current Ethiopian theological controversies.

domestic affairs, the short shrift given to their *abuna* and his disregard of the patriarchal decree, the widespread religious ignorance that inevitably leads to superstitious fanaticism, the annoyance of the theological parties whose pet doctrines were condemned, all contributed to the raising of a furious controversy. Gabra Michael was appalled: instead of bringing peace and truth to his church he had brought more dissension and more bitter quarrelling. In September 1843 he came again to Gondar and tried to get the support of his old master Walda Selassie; he failed. Then he set out towards Adowa alone, and in February 1844 was reconciled by Father Justin de Jacobis with the Catholic Church.

In after years Father de Jacobis wrote of Gabra Michael as 'honest, discerning, energetic, exemplary; a man of genius, who never was contaminated in the slightest degree by the degeneracy of Christianity in his unhappy country, who avoided all sectarianism and sought relentlessly for truth'. He was the very man the Lazarists required in their work: they had a score of young Ethiopians who wanted to be priests, and Gabra Michael was a most valuable auxiliary in their training; with Father de Jacobis he translated a textbook of moral theology into Amharic and drew up a catechism of Christian doctrine adapted to local needs. Together they visited various monasteries, and at Gunde Gunde a number of the monks were reconciled: they brought about the grant to the Lazarists of some of the monastery's land at Guala and a college was established, with Gabra Michael in charge and Takla Haymanot from Gunde Gunde as one of his assistants. Here, in 1846, over a dozen Ethiopian priests were received into communion with Rome.

This was an opportunity for Abuna Salama, still exiled in Tigrai, to stir up feeling against 'the Franks'. The Holy See had recently set up a vicariate apostolic among the

Gallas, with a Capuchin friar, Mgr (afterwards cardinal) Massaia, at its head. Salama professed to excommunicate Massaia, 'the Frankish James' (de Jacobis), Gabra Michael, and all their assistants, forbidding anybody to harbour or help them. When this had no effect at all, he frightened the ruler of Tigrai into banishing the two European leaders, who had to take refuge at Massawa. During their absence the little group of Ethiopian clergy, half in hiding at Alitiena, was troubled by internal disputes, and Gabra Michael was again fired by the vision of bringing peace to the distracted Ethiopian Christians by establishing truth and unity at the centres of dissension throughout the country. He set out with two of his disciples, but Salama was on the watch; they were seized, and spent nearly three months in chains before they were released by order of Ras Ubieh. On their return to Alitiena they found that Justin de Jacobis had returned in defiance of his enemies; at Massawa he had been consecrated bishop by Mgr Massaia, and the first priest that he ordained was Gabra Michael, now sixty years old, sending him immediately afterwards to Gondar, together with Takla Haymanot and an Italian Lazarist named Biancheri.

At first they had an almost startling success. The negus John formally and openly repudiated the heresy and schism of his church, and was followed by many clergy, monks and lay people, including two monks who were delegates of Abuna Salama. Mgr de Jacobis visited the city, and on that occasion received Abba Gabra Michael as a postulant in the Lazarist congregation. But this progress came to a swift and sudden end: within two years an obscure *ras* (chieftain) called Kedaref Kassa had overrun Amhara, Gojjam and Tigrai and proclaimed himself king of kings under the name of Theodore; and he bought the valuable support of Abuna Salama by recalling him and threatening penalties against all who should repudiate

Monophysism. In July 1854, Gabra Michael, Takla Haymanot and three other Ethiopians were arrested and brought before an assembly, presided over by Salama, at which all the clergy of Gondar solemnly rejected Catholicism.[1] Gabra Michael and his companions stood firm and were returned to their dungeon, where their legs were made fast in a horrible wooden vice, a sort of stocks. Three weeks later they were brought before Theodore and confronted with the dethroned negus John, who, after a week of resistance, had just repudiated the faith he had learned from Gabra Michael. They were sorrowful, but still firm.

At intervals over a period of nine months the five were dragged from their filthy cell into the presence of Theodore and Salama to be browbeaten and cajoled; and each time they were lashed with a giraffe's tail (the hair of which is like steel wire) and tortured in other ways, especially by the contraption by which their legs were fastened together. 'In certain matters of faith', Gabra Michael reminded Salama on one of these occasions, 'I cannot be other than opposed to you, but so far as Christian charity is concerned I think I have never done you anything but good'—referring especially to the time when he had persuaded the negus John not to execute the bishop. In March 1855, Theodore set out on an expedition against the ruler of Shoa; he was furious that he had been unable to break Gabra Michael's spirit, and although the old man was worn out by his sufferings he was taken along with the army, in chains. His plight, his patience and his kindliness touched the soldiers—he was still preaching Christ's gospel, and it had its fruit in softening the hearts of rough and careless men. Then, on May 31, a last attempt was made

[1] Including those who had recently professed it. They must not be judged hardly; most of them had done so only because their sovereign did, and not out of any real conviction.

to make him submit to the king by repudiating his faith: again he refused, and was condemned to death.

He managed to send a message to the other confessors at Gondar: 'Be steadfast, even to death. I have no hope of seeing you again on this earth. If they kill me, I shall die testifying to my faith; if they spare me, I shall go on preaching it.'

Among those present was the British consul in Ethiopia, Walter Chichele Plowden, one of the two British supporters and advisers of Theodore. Plowden (who was to be murdered by Theodore's enemies five years later) now came forward with others and begged a reprieve for Gabra Michael. It was granted, though it would have been kinder to let him die, for he was to remain a prisoner in the hands of Theodore. For three more months, completely decrepit with age and ill-treatment, he was dragged from place to place in chains in the train of the king; thirty years before, in the prime of life, he had walked over Ethiopia seeking for truth and the *Book of Monks*: now he was led whither he would not, a living witness to the truth he had learned. He caught cholera, and there was a shortage of food; he gave away his own pittance to other sufferers, and could hardly be persuaded to ride on the mule that somebody got for him.

On 28 August 1855, came release. Abba Gabra Michael lay down by the side of the road and died. The soldiers gently removed his chains and buried his body. He was beatified as a martyr in 1926, thirteen years before his master and father-in-God, Bishop de Jacobis, was beatified as a confessor.

MATTHEW GREGORY NAKKAR
A Syrian Saul

In the history of Christianity there have been several examples of men who, like Saul of Tarsus, fiercely persecuted the faithful of Christ, were touched by the hand of God, and, like Paul, became heralds of that which they had persecuted. The Syrian bishop Matthew Gregory Nakkar was one such only a century ago, but he lived in a now vanished world of the Turkish empire, wherein each religious communion was a separate *millet* ('nation') whose members formed not only a religious but a civil unit, so that he who abandoned the religion was doubly an apostate, a traitor to his people.

Between 1825 and 1830 nearly all the Syrian Jacobites[1] in Damascus and southern Lebanon had, under the leadership of a lay notable, abu-Hamad, and the bishop Jacob al-Haliani, returned to the communion of the Catholic Church: there were, in fact, only fifteen Jacobite families left there. The Jacobite patriarch, ibn-Sayar, was extremely alarmed, and he sent his representative to Damascus to deal with the situation, the first step being to get the bishop Jacob put in prison. This representative was Matthew Nakkar, metropolitan of Mosul in what is now known as Iraq.

Nakkar had been born in 1795 into a distinguished

[1] They derive from the monophysite schism, and are called Jacobites after Jacob Baradai, who organized them in the sixth century.

family which for six hundred years had monopolized the
Jacobite see of Mosul; it was, indeed, called Bait al-
Mutran, the 'Metropolitan House'.[1] At the age of twenty-
five he was ordained priest and made archdeacon, that is,
'vicar general', to his aged uncle, Mar Isso, the then metropolitan, and at once distinguished himself by his zeal
against Catholics of the Syrian rite. In his own words, 'My
hatred for Catholics, inherited from my ancestors, increased every day; I preached against them relentlessly
and formally taught what they regarded as heresy . . . I did
all in my power to hamper their clergy in their ministry. . .
To profess Catholicism seemed to me scandalous and dis-
honourable.'[2] While still a layman he had denounced six
Catholic priests, formerly Jacobites, for ignoring the
sultan's order forbidding change of religion; he had cut off
their hair and beards (the mark of degradation among
Eastern clergy), encouraged a shameless woman to slap
their shaven heads with her slipper, and finally engineered
their expulsion from their town.

In 1826 this young man succeeded Mar Isso as metropolitan of Mosul. Soon afterwards two Jacobite bishops,
Antony Samhiri of Diarbekr and Issa Mahfuz of Jerusalem, became Catholics and, owing to the influence of a
layman named Elias Shadi, were given possession of the
Jacobite church of the Forty Martyrs by the Turkish
governor at Mardin, in northern Mesopotamia.[3] Although
this had not happened in his own diocese, Mar Matthew
at once became very active; he went to a higher authority,

---

[1] The succession was, of course, collateral; Jacobite bishops may not
be married.
[2] *Notice sur la vie de Mgr Matthéo Nakkar*, by himself (Lille, 1851).
[3] It was intrigues of this sort that added so much to the bitterness of
religious strife in the Near East. In this one, as usual, the Catholics
appealed for the support of the French consul, and got it, and so
made matters worse.

Daud Pasha at Baghdad, and, for a suitable consideration, got an order for the imprisonment of the two bishops, the arrest of Shadi when he could be found, and the return to the Jacobites of their church. He was so anxious to announce his success to the metropolitan of Mardin that, he says, 'I did the journey from Baghdad to Mardin in eight days instead of the usual leisurely twenty-five; I was the death of eighteen horses!' It was Matthew's success in this business that caused his patriarch to send him to Damascus.

But when he arrived there he found that the bird he was after had flown: Bishop Jacob al-Haliani had prudently betaken himself to the Maronites in the Lebanon, and the most that Mar Matthew could achieve was to get twenty-five Catholic Syrians imprisoned for the like number of days. He also got the Turkish governor to write to the Maronite emir, the great Bashir Shihab, who ruled for over fifty years, ordering him to give up Mar Jacob: Bashir's letter in reply was most polite and full of the floweriest compliments—but it made no reference to the subject of the correspondence.[1]After that Matthew decided to give up for the present, and he went to Jerusalem for Holy Week.

In the church of the Holy Sepulchre it is the custom on Easter eve for the Orthodox patriarch and an Armenian ecclesiastic to shut themselves up in the chapel of the Angel before the sepulchre, kindle fire, and pass it out through small windows to the waiting multitude outside. This is not the place to give an account of the history and significance of this ceremony:[2] it is sufficient to say that

[1] For centuries the Maronites were an ever-ready refuge for persecuted Catholics of all rites; though subjects of the sultan of Turkey, they were practically autonomous under their own emirs and protected by their craggy mountains.

[2] See for instance, R. Curzon's *Visits to Monasteries of the Levant*,

many Christians in Jerusalem still believed that this 'holy fire' came down miraculously from Heaven (and some of their clergy were not so active as they might have been to disabuse their minds). This belief was not confined to the simpler sort of folk: Matthew Nakkar, for example, firmly believed in the miracle and all that he had heard about the properties of the holy fire, e.g., that it did not burn. Accordingly on this Easter eve of 1832 he went with his deacon to the church, joined in the procession, united his heart with that of the excited crowd, and jostled with them to light his candle at the holy fire. With triumph he turned to his deacon and, to demonstrate the miracle, applied the flame to the deacon's long beard—it disappeared in a flash of light, sizzling and smelling. 'I cannot express my amazement,' wrote Mar Matthew, 'I was so certain that the fire would not burn that for a few minutes I was stupefied: then I pulled myself together and bitterly reproached my deacon for his lack of faith that had caused his beard to be burnt!' This shock was the beginning of the change in Matthew Nakkar's life: he had firmly believed the holy fire to be an annual miracle by which God set his approval on these churches which were separated from Rome, and now he knew it was no miracle; henceforward he began to have other doubts, and he resolved to make a study of those points of religion about which there is disagreement between the Jacobites and the Catholic Church.

Meanwhile he was sent by his patriarch to Aleppo, to execute an order from the Turkish government banishing the Catholic Syrians from the town and depriving them of their church. They were a numerous body. When Mar Matthew had passed through Aleppo on his way to Damascus they had met him in procession and accom-

---

part II, cap. 4, and for a later account H. C. Luke's *Ceremonies at the Holy Places* (London and Milwaukee, 1932).

panied him with every mark of respect to their church, the object of this courtesy being not only to put themselves in the good books of the persecuting bishop (as they admitted afterwards), but also to delay him while they sent a messenger to warn Mar Jacob at Damascus. Now Nakkar would show them that they had failed in the first of their objects, even if they had succeeded in the second. The Turkish governor of Aleppo received the imperial *firman* from the bishop with all respect, but explained that the Moslem fast of Ramadan was then on and the sultan's orders could not be put into effect till it was over: his lordship would therefore have to wait.

So Mar Matthew sent his servant to find accommodation in some quiet place; he did not want to advertise his presence in Aleppo, for if the suspicions of the Catholics were aroused they might be able to collect a larger *baksheesh* than the Jacobite patriarch had paid and induce an official to get the decree revoked. In due course his servant conducted him to the Khan al-Banadika, 'Venetian Inn', on the outskirts of the town, where he was received with great courtesy and given the best room in the house. It was only when he was installed there that Mar Matthew discovered that the 'Venetian Inn' was not an inn at all, but the house of the French Lazarists. 'I must admit that I was extremely frightened. Here was I, come to Aleppo to persecute Catholics, lodged in a Latin monastery. The least inconvenient thing that could happen would be that the Syrian Catholics would hear of my presence in the town, which was the very thing I wanted to avoid.'

The superior of the Lazarists, Father Nicholas Godès, had a shock, too, when he learned that the terror of Syria was a guest under his roof. But he was not frightened—on the contrary, he was pleased; and he treated his visitor with such respect and friendliness that Mar Matthew soon confided to him the doubts that had disturbed his mind since his visit to Jerusalem. Conversations and discussions followed, which turned principally on Monophysism: was Jesus Christ a real, whole and complete man as well as God, or was he not? Matthew found that his views were less easy to defend than he had supposed—he was particularly impressed by the testimonies that Father Godès adduced from the writings of the Syrian doctor St Ephrem, and he asked permission to read for himself in the Lazarists' library. He read there and he prayed; Matthew the persecutor was an honest man and he was really worried—so much so that, he tells us, he began to lose his appetite. But his way was being made more and more clear, and on 27 November 1832, in the church at Aleppo that he had come to recover, he made a public abjuration of heresy and was reconciled by the patriarch of the Catholic Syrians, Mar Gregory (Jarwah).

Then the persecutor became the persecuted. He went straight to Mardin, the chief Jacobite stronghold, and preached in the church of the Catholic Armenians: within two months, fifty-four Jacobites had formally abandoned their errors. The Jacobite patriarch cited him before the governor, accusing him of receiving 'a chest of gold' from the pope as the price of his apostasy, and of enticing good Jacobites from their allegiance to the sultan to that of the 'Franks'. The governor asked Matthew why he had repudiated his own patriarch in favour of the pope.

'Excellency,' he replied, 'in former times all Christians were united in one faith and recognized one ultimate religious head on earth, the pope. Through error and ignorance the Jacobites were separated from this unity. I have returned to it.'

'That seems to me quite harmless,' was the governor's observation on this, but the patriarch insisted.

"Excellency, in the interests of the peace of my *millet*,[1] I must ask that this man be put in prison. Otherwise I shall have to inform his imperial majesty of the lukewarmness with which you obey his orders.'

This disturbed the governor, and Matthew was imprisoned, first in the common jail and then in the monastery of Zafaran. Here he was in the power of the ruthless patriarch, who sought to force him into apostasy. For a fortnight he was confined in an empty underground cistern —just such a thing as that into which Joseph was cast by his brethren (Genesis 37: 24)—and every evening he was drawn out and cruelly beaten. Then he was brought before the patriarch in his house, dressed in a caricature of episcopal vestments (in reference to the pastoral staff and the rest that had been sent him by Pope Gregory XVI), and ordered to curse the Council of Chalcedon. He refused. Thereupon he was struck in the mouth, the blow breaking his teeth, and was literally kicked from the top of a flight of steps to the bottom. He lay there unable to move. He was picked up and flung into a hut outside the monastery. 'If he dies,' was the order, 'throw his body to the dogs.'

What happened next may be told in Matthew's own words—it sounds rather like an episode from the *Arabian Nights*.

'The next morning, while I was praying to God with all my heart to give me strength, a Kurdish princess whose husband was staying at Zafaran happened to pass the hut and heard my groans. She asked a bystander to open the door (which had been locked) and when he said he dare not for fear of the patriarch she told her servants to break it down. . . When she heard my story she sent for her husband, who had me taken to one of his rooms and there for two weeks I was treated with the greatest care and

---

[1] Of which he was the civil as well as the religious head, and responsible to the state.

kindness. My clothes were in rags, so I was given some of the prince's, and when the prince left Zafaran he sent me back to Mardin in the care of his son, the emir Ahmad, with instructions to the governor that I and all other Catholics were to be properly treated and protected.'

Mar Matthew returned to his preaching and teaching with more zeal than ever; at the end of a year he had won over his own successor in the see of Mosul, the metropolitan of Mardin itself, a number of lower clergy and a thousand lay people. Then the Catholic patriarch made him bishop of Nabk and Kariatim, a diocese adjoining that of Homs in Syria, which did not contain a single Catholic. Here he worked for many years under conditions of the greatest difficulty and with a success that provoked the Jacobites, and through them the Moslems, to increase the difficulties. He wrote in 1849: 'As for the diocese of which I am bishop, it has had its share of hardships and misfortunes from this cruel war.[1] My own property has been pillaged and my house sacked; two of my best priests have had their throats cut and their house was burnt down. . . Most of the faithful have lost all their little and we are, all of us, reduced to utter poverty. In and around Kariatim there are 18,000 Catholic Syrians and not a single church: the Holy Offering has to be celebrated in a small room, which of course means that most of them can only take part in it from outside.' Very shortly after he was able to obtain recognition of his flock from the imperial government, which meant that they received legal rights against their persecutors and were free to build churches.

Mar Matthew was taken seriously ill early in 1868,

---

[1] Local warfare consequent on the attempt of the Turks to abolish the semi-autonomy of the Maronites and Druzes in the Lebanon. It was characteristic of the time and place that when Mar Matthew travelled about his diocese he had to be accompanied by horsemen armed with swords and muskets.

when he was seventy-three. He went for treatment to Beirut and then returned to his diocese, but his case was hopeless and he retired to the Syrian ecclesiastical college at Sharfeh, where he fell asleep in the Lord on 22 March 1868. His tomb is in the college chapel.

THREE MARONITE
RELIGIOUS
*Namatallah al-Hardini, Monk. Sharbel of
Beqaa-Kafra, Hermit. Rafqa ar-Rais, Nun*

The people called Maronites are a body of Syrians who
form the principal community in the republic of Lebanon;
ecclesiastically, they derive ultimately from the same source
as the Catholic Syrians, having a form of the Antiochene
rites of worship, but they are organized quite separately.
Their origin as a separate people with their own church
organization is probably to be looked for in Bait Marun,
a monastery built round the shrine of St Maro, a fifth-
century hermit, on the river Orontes near Homs, and it is
therefore specially fitting that the monastic life should
always have had many followers among the Maronite
people. In chapter xiii of the second volume of his *Arabia
Deserta*, C. M. Doughty gives a vivid account of a visit he
paid to a Maronite monastery in the Lebanon some eighty
years ago. He speaks of its lovely situation and of the
austere, hard-working lives of the monks and of their
offices in the church, and narrates his conversation with a
young priest, the guestmaster.

This priest, he says, 'seeing me suffer from rheumatism
in the autumn clouds of these high places, exhorted me,
with an affectionate humility, to visit one of the saints, the
distance to whose convent was only five little hours, and
he would ask his abbot's leave to accompany me. One of

those men of God healed all manner of infirmities... This young priest was epileptic, from a child; and "had been wont," he said, "to fall every day once, till he went to the saint, with whom he abode four months; and the malady left him." ' Doughty also records that the said young priest did not know whether King Solomon and St Ephrem lived before or after the earthly days of Christ, and thought there was no wine in the world before our Lord made it at the Cana marriage-feast, and asked in what part of the world Mount Sinai lay, and other curious and unlikely pieces of ignorance.

Doughty does not give the name of the monastery which he visited on this occasion but it was in fact one dedicated in honour of St Antony the Great at Qoshayya. It is first mentioned in a document of the year 1104, and another, dated 1215, states that it was the see of the first Maronite bishops. It has belonged to the Lebanese (or Baladite) congregation of Maronite Antonians since 1708. The present church was built not long before the time that Doughty visited it, and the rest of the buildings were just as he saw them until 1926, when the two upper storeys were rebuilt.

The young newly-ordained monk with whom Doughty talked has been identified as Father Peter Kaitu, and there were monks recently living who knew him in his old age. They were at a loss to understand some of the things that Doughty reports of his conversation. As the venerable Father Martin Tarabey, abbot general of the Baladites, remarked when his attention was drawn to the passage in *Arabia Deserta*, 'It is true that our monks were simple folk in those days, but they were neither simpletons nor crassly ignorant.' Moreover, Father Peter was remembered as a man of particular intelligence and talent. It has been suggested that Doughty had an insufficient command of the Lebanese dialect of Arabic; that Father Peter was poking fun at the strange Englishman is perhaps more likely.

Doughty's general account of Qoshayya was very exact, but he misunderstood what Father Peter said about the cure of his epilepsy. This was not brought about by the hermit whom he wanted Doughty to see about his rheumatism, but at the tomb of Father Namatallah al-Hardini.

This monk was born in 1808, at Hardin in the Batrun district and was christened Joseph: his father was a peasant named George Kassab. Schools were few and far between in Syria in those days, but Joseph had a lively mind under a quiet exterior, and his father made a special effort to send the boy for a time to a monastery near Tannurin, where there was an elementary school. Here Joseph learned to read and write his vernacular Arabic, and also began Syriac, the liturgical language of the Maronite rite. Then he returned home, and for some years helped his father in the fields.

But he had made up his mind to be a monk, and when he was twenty was received into the community of Qoshayya, taking the name of Namatallah, to which al-Hardini was added in reference to his birthplace. He was a model neophyte, and after two years was sent to study for the priesthood at the monastery of St Cyprian at Kfifan. Here his zeal outran his discretion, he overworked and got himself into that distressing spiritual state called scrupulosity. His studies had to be dropped for a time and his abbot sent him for a rest to the monastery of Mar Musa al-Habashi (St Moses the Ethiop); here he worked in the tailor's shop and made a good recovery, so that by the age of twenty-five he was able to be ordained priest.

The life of an Antonian monk is not calculated to be eventful, and Father Namatallah provides no exception: his biographer and namesake, Father Namatallah al-Kafri, has to fall back on the old hagiographical device of writing a sort of miniature treatise on the Christian virtues around his subject, which results in a picture that one would expect to be more or less true of any ordinarily good and observant religious. It does not appear that Father Namatallah was sent out to any of the parishes for which the Maronite monks are responsible but led an entirely claustral life: he continued to work with the tailors, and also became a skilled binder of books. He suffered a good deal from ill-health, and was one of those unfortunate people who 'feel the cold', which in the Lebanon is intense in winter: Maronite monks wear sandals, which are not the most comforting of footgear in an unheated church. Pursuing his own quiet way Father Namatallah gained the love and respect and then the veneration of his brethren. There was talk of his being made *rais* (superior) of a house or even abbot general of the congregation. 'I would rather die!' he exclaimed, when it came to his ears. Someone suggested that it might be God's will that he should be abbot general. 'Not at all,' said Father Namatallah, 'His will is that I should not.'

'How do you know?' he was asked.

'Because he told me so.'

Evidently Father Namatallah was not one of those religious people, all too common, who believe that the will of God is necessarily that which cuts across one's own inclination.

But though he did in fact escape the office of abbot general he served as one of the four assistants of the general, and infused much of his own devoted spirit into all parts of the Baladite congregation. He was also for six years in charge of the young students at Kfifan and was thus in a position directly to form and encourage the rising generation of monks.

At the beginning of December 1858 Father Namatallah was attacked by pleurisy. The bitter north winds that were sweeping the mountains at the time aggravated his complaint, and after acute suffering he died peacefully on

December 14. When some time later his body was removed
from the ground to be reburied within the church at Kfifan,
it was found to be still incorrupt, and his tomb rapidly
became a place of pilgrimage. Many unusual occurrences
have been recorded there, of which one may be mentioned,
that of the Father Peter Kaitu already referred to in connection with C. M. Doughty. He was, as has been said, an
epileptic. One day in 1869, while praying at the tomb of
Father Namatallah he was seized by a fit of more than
ordinary violence, and it was the last one that he ever had.

Among the monks who gathered round the deathbed of
Father Namatallah al-Hardini was a Brother Sharbel, who
had been born into a peasant family thirty years before at
Beqaa-Kafra, the highest inhabited place in Lebanon, near
the famous cedars. He was christened Joseph and, having
lost his father in babyhood, responsibility for him was
shared by his mother and his uncle, Tanios Makhluf. Two
other uncles were hermits, and the influence of these on
the growing boy was strong. In due course he heard a call
to the religious life and, fearing his relatives would object
(for all that they were devout folk), he left home secretly
and presented himself at the monastery of our Lady of
Mayfuq. His uncle was sent to fetch Joseph back, but it
was to no purpose, and he was admitted to the community,
taking the name of a Syrian martyr, Sharbel. That had been
in 1851, when he was twenty-three. At the time of Father
Namatallah's death he was finishing his theology at Kfifan,
and in the following year was ordained priest and took up
his residence at the monastery of St Maro at Annaya,
which is over 3,500 feet above the sea, in the district of
Gibail.

Father Sharbel lived in this community for fifteen years
and was a model monk in the exact sense of the word: it is
recorded that, though he rejoiced to be able to be of the
slightest assistance to his neighbour, nevertheless it was

Father Sharbel

Father Sharbel's Hermitage at Annaya

always a trial to him to have to leave his monastery to go
to some neighbouring village to transact some business or
'to pray over the head of a sick man'. It was his delight to
pass his time in singing the office in choir, in working in
the fields and in reading—his favourite book was the
Imitation of Christ—and nobody was surprised when
eventually he asked, and received, the permission of his
rais to go and live in a hermitage that had become vacant.

It must be understood that whereas on the one hand
many Maronite monks are engaged in parochial and
pastoral work, provision is made on the other hand for a
few chosen souls to lead an eremitical life (generally in
twos). The hermitage to which Father Sharbel went was
called SS Peter and Paul's, and had been built in 1798,
some years before the monastery itself, by two well-off
villagers who had spent the rest of their lives there; it consisted of four tiny rooms or cells, and a small chapel.
Father Sharbel had been preceded by Father Elisha al-
Hardini, who had lived forty-four years in the hermitage.
The communal life of a Maronite monk is sufficiently
hard, involving perpetual abstinence from flesh meat and
tobacco, four periods of fasting in the year, and night office
at midnight; but the hermit has to fast all the year round,
without meat, fruit or wine; he must join manual work to
his prayer; speech must be kept to a minimum, and he
may not go away from the hermitage without express permission. Father Sharbel's bed was a mattress stuffed with
leaves, laid on the floor and covered with goatskin, the
pillow a block of wood wrapped in a piece of an old habit;
and he put himself under obedience to the other hermit
with him. In these and other ways he carried on in the
nineteenth century the life of the early desert fathers,
whose lives he read and re-read. Like so many of them, he
found his solitude broken by visitors who had heard of him
as a very holy man; they came from all over southern

Lebanon, to ask his advice or prayers or simply for a blessing, and of course some came out of mere curiosity, especially after it was noised abroad that through him God gave miracles. Then there were added to his visitors many sick folk who came seeking a cure, and some were cured.

Father Sharbel lived thus for twenty-three years, his austerities seeming to increase the robustness of his health. Then one morning, in the middle of December 1898, he was taken ill without warning, just before the consecration while celebrating the Liturgy; Father Makarios, who was serving him, induced him to leave the altar till he felt able to continue, but when he reached the point where, with the chalice in his hand, there is said the prayer beginning, 'Father of truth, behold your Son, who makes atoning sacrifice to you', he found he was unable to replace the chalice on the altar. Father Makarios gently disengaged his fingers, put the chalice down for him, and led him to his cell. He never got up from his bed again; the paralysis gradually gained on him, he was anointed, and Father Makarios took it in turns with the parish priest to sit with him day and night. They read to and prayed with him, but at times he lost consciousness and on the night of Christmas eve he died, repeating the prayer which he had been unable to finish at the altar: 'Father of truth, behold your Son, who makes atoning sacrifice to you. Accept the offering; he died for me that I might have life. Behold the offering! Accept it . . .' The words figured Father Sharbel's own life of seventy years.

Some years later the *rais* of Annaya obtained permission from the patriarch Elias Hoyek to disinter the body of Father Sharbel and transfer it to a chapel. It was found that in spite of the wetness of the grave the body was still incorrupt, without any smell of decay and exuding a sort of fluid. These phenomena have continued, and were verified when the new tomb was reopened in 1952.

Three Maronite Religious

At the time of the massacres in 1860 there was living in Lebanon a young Maronite nun named Rafqa (Rebecca) ar-Rais. She was at Dair al-Qamar when the monastery there was attacked, and she was the means of saving the life of a Christian lad. He was being pursued by men, Druzes or Turkish soldiers, with muskets and bayonets, and when he saw the nun he ran to her for refuge. She threw her cloak about him, and, thus concealed, the fanatics passed him by unseen. This cool-headed young woman was born of a poor family in a remote village, and for years could not read or write; but she left an account in her own words of the first part of her long life, an account very touching in its simplicity.

'I was baptized Petra, at Hemlaya, near Bikfaya in Lebanon. I lost my mother when I was seven years old. My father married again two years later.

'When I was fourteen my stepmother wanted me to marry her brother, but my aunt wanted me to marry her son, my cousin. They used to quarrel about this. When I could no longer bear to hear them abusing one another, I asked God to help me out of the difficulty. Then it occurred to me I would be a nun. I went off at once to the Maryamat sisters at their convent of our Lady of Help at Bikfaya. The mother superior received me kindly.

'The next day my father arrived with his wife to fetch me home. I implored the reverend mother not to make me see them. I told her I would rather join my mother in the grave than go back home. My father went away very glumly, and I have not seen him since.

'After two years' trial I received the religious habit, and I was sent to the Ghazir convent, where I was put in charge of the kitchen. In my spare time I learned to read and write and figure. After that I was sent to several schools, at Bait-Shahib, Shuwayr, Hammana and elsewhere. During the massacres in 1860 I was at Dair al-Qamar. . . Then I was sent to Ma'ad, where I spent seven years teaching a class of more than sixty pupils.'

At this time there was a rumour that the Jesuit fathers, who directed the Maryamat, were going to dissolve the congregation. (It did not happen, and the Maryamat are still flourishing in Lebanon and Syria.) Sister Rafqa, as Petra was now called, goes on:

'This news made me very sad, for I did not want ever to return to the world. Not knowing what to do, I went into St George's church at Ma'ad. Kneeling before the altar, I suddenly felt weak and lost consciousness. And I saw, as if in a dream, three people—a white-bearded monk leaning on a stick, a soldier and an old man. The monk touched me with his staff and said, "Go to the Antonian nuns!" On my way back to the school I met one of the important men of the town, Antony Issa. I told him my troubles and about the vision, and he did his best to cheer me up. He took me home with him and wrote a letter of recommendation to the authorities of the Antonian nuns, and he also promised to give me a dowry.

'With complete trust in God, I went to the convent of St Simeon al-Qarneh, near Ehden in northern Lebanon. I was received among the novices and a year later, in 1872, was given the veil.

'Up till then I had always had good health, never being the least bit ailing. And one Sunday, praying before the Blessed Sacrament, I said to God, "Lord, why do you ignore your servant? Why don't you send her some sickness? Have you forgotten her?"

'That night at bed-time I had a frightful headache, which led to my present blindness. I must not complain, because I asked for it.'

There ends Sister Rafqa's own story. She continued to

suffer greatly in her head, and her sight got worse and worse. No doctor could do anything for her. After ten years she became totally blind, and this state seems to have been finally hastened by the clumsiness of an American doctor to whom she had been sent. Sister Rafqa simply thanked him.

When she was sixty-four a new affliction came to her: she was reduced to a state of almost complete physical helplessness. 'But I can still use my tongue to praise God,' she said, 'and my hands, to prevent me from being idle.' She had to lie in bed all day, knitting stockings, welcoming with a brilliant smile the sisters who came to see her and edifying them by her extraordinary patience and courage.

And already inexplicable things were happening. On the eve of one Corpus Christi Rafqa said she wanted to come to Mass next day. 'Of course you can't,' said the abbess, 'you'll have to pray in bed as usual.' But next morning she was in choir. When asked how she got there she replied, 'I don't know, I just stretched my legs, got out of bed, and slipped down to church.' Another time, when asked if she didn't wish she could see her sisters and the room she was in, she said, 'Yes, I should like to see you all for a few minutes.' Shortly afterwards she said with a smile, 'I'm beginning to see. Look, there are two books on the table—the Bible and the *Lives of the Saints*.' And she did indeed recover her sight for a little time. Two nuns who were present on that occasion, Sister Angela Huwayek and Sister Marina Sader, were still living a few years ago.

Sister Rafqa died at the convent of St Joseph at Grabta in 1914; she was eighty-one years old. Four days after her funeral a strange radiance was said to be seen above her grave, lighting up the leaves of the oak-tree that overshadowed it. Soon miraculous cures were reported at her intercession, and they have continued to this day.

Three Maronite victims of the 1860 massacres, the

brothers Francis, Abdulmuti and Raphael Masabki, all laymen, have already been beatified; it is hoped that before long Namatallah al-Hardini, Sharbel Makhluf and Rafqa ar-Rais will join them in the Maronite calendar. Their causes have been introduced at Rome, that of Father Sharbel having made the most progress. During the past thirty years very many healings at his intercession have been reported, and pilgrims flock to his tomb at Annaya in their thousands, Moslems as well as Christians of all communions; they come from all over the Near East and even from western Europe and America.

718

Attwater

Saints of the East.

HOLLAND

A
Enlargement of the Bosporus area.

Black Sea

Constantinople
Chrysopolis
Chalcedon
Bosporus

Sea of Marmara

ASIA MINOR

Nicaea

FRANCE

Venice
San Lazzaro

R. Danube

Trno

Studenitsa
Edidaurus
Nova Pazar

BULGARI

Podgoritsa

MACEDONIA

Phillippi

Rome
Grottaferrata
Vallelucio
Monte Cassino

Apulia

Mt. Athos

Thessalonika

ITALY

Calabria

GRE

San Demetrio Corone

SICILY

Athens

C. Passaro

Modon

Mediterranean Sea

Asmara
Massawa

Tigrai
Alitiena
Aksum
Adowa

Red Sea

ARABIA

LIBY

Gondar

Amhara

Gulf of Aden

DESE

White Nile

Blue Nile

Gojjam

Shoa

Addis Ababa

ETHIOPIA

ETHIOPIA
on same scale